PRAYERS & PROMISES
for First
Responders

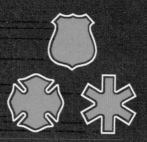

Adam Davis and
Lt. Col. Dave Grossman

BroadStreet
PUBLISHING

BroadStreet Publishing® Group, LLC
Savage, Minnesota, USA
BroadStreetPublishing.com

Prayers & Promises for First Responders

978-1-4245-6278-7 (faux leather)
978-1-4245-6279-4 (e-book)

Stock or custom editions of BroadStreet Publishing titles may be purchased in bulk for educational, business, ministry, fundraising, or sales promotional use. For information, please email orders@broadstreetpublishing.com.

Published in association with Cyle Young of the Hartline Literary Agency, LLC.
Cover and interior by Garborg Design at GarborgDesign.com

Printed in China

21 22 23 24 25   5 4 3 2 1

DEDICATION

This book is dedicated to all of the men and women who serve communities in our nation—from coast to coast and from sea to shining sea. For the police officer, the firefighter, the emergency medical technician, and everyone behind the scenes. May you find peace and comfort in your times of need, an encouraging word for moments when you're feeling down, and a challenging thought to draw you closer to God. This book is for you in honor of your unrelenting service to our nation.

THEMES

INTRODUCTION

All books are not created equal. Each has a life of its own and a unique purpose. Within the pages of this book, you will find encouraging Scripture passages. But before you proceed, we would also like you to understand what we hope you will experience as you read. While moving through the book, set aside time to dig into the Scripture and study it within context. For example, if you see a particular Scripture verse that inspires you, read the chapter in which it's found and learn more about the history of the verse, the cultural background, and the meaning of keywords in the original text. In short, we suggest reading it as follows:

1. Read the devotional entries.
2. Contemplate the message in prayer.
3. Read the applicable Scripture verses.
4. Study them within their context to understand the deeper meaning.

In times of hardship and adversity, we must rely and stand on the foundation of God's Word. Trials will come, trouble will undoubtedly arise, but the promises of God are forever. Stand on his promises and use these prompts to become a devoted student of God's Word.

ABANDONMENT

Life presents us with challenges, and many are difficult to overcome. One such challenge is that of abandonment. Biological parents abandon their children, spouses abandon spouses, friends abandon friends, and agencies and fellow brothers and sisters abandon first responders. This world has nothing good in it except those who are followers of Christ and doing the work of his kingdom. Even on the cross Jesus cried out, "My God, my God, why have you forsaken me?" (Matthew 27:46 NIV). Sin permanently separates humanity from God, but Jesus restored that separation. It was sin that Jesus bore on the cross for all humankind, for all time. If others abandon you, rest assured that no matter what you face in life, Jesus will not abandon you. That is perfect peace and a blessed assurance of hope and comfort in Christ.

Heavenly Father, my life is not my own. I know to live is Christ, and to die is gain. If others abandon me and if the world forsakes me, I cling to you. Be present in all my circumstances. Amen.

How can you incorporate these passages into your life as reminders of the ever-present help of God?

Even if my father and mother abandon me,
the LORD will hold me close.

PSALMS 27:10 NLT

LORD, do not forsake me;
do not be far from me, my God.

PSALMS 38:21 NIV

Don't love money; be satisfied with what you have.
For God has said, "I will never fail you.
I will never abandon you."

HEBREWS 13:5 NLT

Persecuted, but not abandoned;
struck down, but not destroyed.

2 CORINTHIANS 4:9 NIV

ASSURANCE

Assurance from the wrong source can provide us with a false sense of security. What a blessed assurance it is to know that Jesus paid the price for our redemption, and all we must do is accept it, embrace it, and live it, and the Word of God will change everything about who we are! The assurance of our salvation is most often debated when we consider a life negotiated with sin instead of surrendered to Christ. Our assurance is simple, and it is this: Jesus came, he died, he rose, and he lives. And in this, by this, and through this, we have eternal life, so long as we confess his name, surrender our lives to his leading, and allow his Word to change our hearts and minds. Rest today in the perfect assurance that our heavenly Father will never change his love for us, and the door is always open to talk to him. He's made a way for us to have eternal life. Will you accept it?

Heavenly Father, when my heart is shaken, let your unfailing love and perfect sacrifice be a reminder of the assurance I need—that as Christ lives in me, I have the assurance for eternity. Amen.

What do you believe is the greatest step we can take to receive assurance of eternal life?

The work of righteousness shall be peace; and the effect of righteousness quietness and assurance for ever.

ISAIAH 32:17 KJV

Faith is confidence in what we hope for and assurance about what we do not see.

HEBREWS 11:1 NIV

We know, brothers and sisters loved by God, that he has chosen you.

1 THESSALONIANS 1:4 NIV

Christ will make his home in your hearts as you trust in him. Your roots will grow down into God's love and keep you strong.

EPHESIANS 3:17 NLT

ATONEMENT

Blood in our veins gives us life. Blood on sacrificial altars in the Old Testament was provided for the sins of people, to purify them and make them right with God. But once and for all, a perfect atonement for sin was made when God sent his only Son, Jesus, to die for all of humanity. The Father made the way for all of us to have a relationship with him through his Son, Jesus. That's the power of atonement. Imagine having to make regular animal sacrifices, like in the Old Testament, and how blessed we are with the life of Jesus. Our response to this atonement should be lives of daily sacrifice, devotion, surrender, and alignment with the Word of God.

Heavenly Father, today I thank you for the perfect atoning blood of your Son, Jesus, and what it means for me. I can have eternal life, and all my sin is washed clean because of this blessed atonement. Help me to live a life worthy of this perfect sacrifice. Amen.

In what ways can your life honor the perfect
sacrifice of atonement made for our sins?

The life of a creature is in the blood, and I have given it
to you to make atonement for yourselves on the altar;
it is the blood that makes atonement for one's life.

LEVITICUS 17:11 NIV

It behoved him to be made like unto his brethren,
that he might be a merciful and faithful high priest
in things pertaining to God, to make reconciliation
for the sins of the people.

HEBREWS 2:17 KJV

Unfailing love and faithfulness make atonement for sin.
By fearing the LORD, people avoid evil.

PROVERBS 16:6 NLT

Iniquities prevail against me;
As for our transgressions,
You will provide atonement for them.

PSALM 65:3 NKJV

AUTHORITY

Without a doubt, those in authority have abused their positions in every venue of our society: politics, church, family, and the workplace. Possessing authority doesn't necessarily mean that you are in a powerful position, and it is certainly not a license to lord control over other people. It is a requirement to be an example to those around you. If you are a husband or wife, submit to each other out of reverence for Christ. Lead biblically. If you hold a leadership position in your workplace or local church, accept the responsibility that comes with it and hold yourself accountable for your actions. To be a biblical leader who leads with humility under the authority of the Great Shepherd means you abide by the Word of God and lead accordingly. It's not permission to be heavy-handed or domineering. No biblical authority comes without great responsibility and accountability for all actions and behaviors. Whether your authority is in the home, in the church, or in the world, use that authority biblically and be an example that honors God.

Heavenly Father, guide me in all I am tasked with today and help me exercise authority that honors you and leads others to a closer walk with you. Amen.

How can biblical authority empower you
to be a more effective servant leader in life?

I give you the authority to trample on serpents and
scorpions, and over all the power of the enemy, and
nothing shall by any means hurt you.
LUKE 10:19 NKJV

At the name of Jesus every knee should bow, of those in
heaven, and of those on earth, and of those under the
earth, and that every tongue should confess that Jesus
Christ is Lord, to the glory of God the Father.
PHILIPPIANS 2:10–11 ESV

Amazement gripped the audience, and they began to
discuss what had happened. "What sort of new teaching
is this?" they asked excitedly. "It has such authority!
Even evil spirits obey his orders!"
MARK 1:27 NLT

Submit yourselves, then, to God.
Resist the devil, and he will flee from you.
JAMES 4:7 NIV

He called his twelve disciples together, and gave them
power and authority over all devils, and to cure diseases.
LUKE 9:1 KJV

BELIEF

If you say, "I believe in airplanes," but you've never boarded a plane, then your level of belief is merely intellectual. You know about airplanes, you have seen them fly, and you know they exist, but you have continued driving long distances instead of utilizing the very resource that you believe in. That's the power of belief in God's Word. We must not only believe in the information he provides in his Word, but we must also believe in our hearts and accept that truth as life-changing. We must allow the truth of his Word to affect how we think, speak, and act. Even demons believe Jesus was born, died, and resurrected. Even demons believe in the Bible, but they do not have life-changing faith. Belief is an element of faith, but belief must be more than intellectual. It must affect our thoughts, our words, and every aspect of our lives. Center your life on what you believe, and place your belief in the truth of God's Word. Let it change you!

Heavenly Father, for every moment I merely believed with my mind but not my heart, I ask for your forgiveness. I believe. I submit not only my mind to you but also my entire life. Amen.

How can daily Bible study help you develop a stronger, deeper understanding of God's Word, thus developing an enduring belief in him?

Jesus said to him, "If you can believe, all things are possible to him who believes."

MARK 9:23 NKJV

Jesus shouted out passionately, "To believe in me is to also believe in God who sent me. For when you look at me you are seeing the One who sent me. I have come as a light to shine in this dark world so that all who trust in me will no longer wander in darkness."

JOHN 12:44–46 TPT

Jesus told him, "Because you have seen me, you have believed; blessed are those who have not seen and yet have believed."

JOHN 20:29 NIV

The Scriptures encourage us with these words: "Everyone who believes in him will never be disappointed."

ROMANS 10:11 TPT

I have written these things to you who believe in the name of the Son of God, so that you may know that you have eternal life.

1 JOHN 5:13 HCSB

BELONGING

In a society where we are "connected" through digital platforms such as social media, smartphones, virtual meetings, texting, and more, we are more disconnected than ever before. In a 2018 study by Cigna,[1] three out of five Americans reported feeling lonely, and only about twenty-five percent feel like they belong or that others understand them. Doesn't it feel good to know that we have a heavenly Father who accepts us as we are, loves us through it all, and sticks by our side regardless of what life throws at us? Belonging isn't found in social trends; it's found in sticking to what you believe in, being vulnerable with those you love, and being present in the moment with your family. God's Word sets the standard for belonging, and he calls those who believe in him his own. Know who you are, where you belong, and whom you belong to.

Heavenly Father, help me remember that you are always near. Remind me through your Word that I am never alone and that I can find true belonging in relationship with you and relationships with other believers. Amen.

1   "New Cigna Study Reveals Loneliness at Epidemic Levels in America," Cigna, Multivu, May 01, 2018, https://www.multivu.com.

How does adhering to the Word of God properly align your priorities for healthy belonging in this life?

> You will be My people,
> and I will be your God.
>
> JEREMIAH 30:22 HCSB

However, your real source of joy isn't merely that these spirits submit to your authority, but that your names are written in the journals of heaven and that you belong to God's kingdom. This is the true source of your authority.

LUKE 10:20 TPT

Jesus, the Holy One, makes us holy. And as sons and daughters, we now belong to his same Father, so he is not ashamed or embarrassed to introduce us as his brothers and sisters!

HEBREWS 2:11 TPT

BLESSING

Blessing is all about perspective. What one person deems a blessing, someone else may take for granted. We are blessed with the ability to breathe, with our lives, our sight, physical strength, health, well-being, the ability to work, and simple things like hugging friends and family. It's not the size of the blessing that quantifies it as a blessing, but it's the perception of the recipient. But blessing is multifaceted. You are a blessing, your work is a blessing, and your life is a blessing. God has blessed us, and we should live in a way that blesses him. In Numbers 6, the Lord instructs Moses how other priests were to bless the Israelites. It begins with this single line: "The LORD bless you and keep you" (6:24 ESV). The word *bless* means to show favor in every area of your life. To *keep* means to protect from harm. When we put our hope in God and see life from his perspective, we begin to see many blessings that were once hidden. Don't allow the battles of life to jade your perspective and cause you to miss out on the best God has for you.

Heavenly Father, thank you for the many blessings in my life, both known and unknown, seen and unseen. Help me to keep my eyes on you, keep my perspective pure, to live to be a blessing, because I am truly blessed beyond measure. Amen.

The more you look for something, the more you will see it. How does knowing the blessings present in your life shift your perspective?

God, your God, has blessed you in everything you have done. He has guarded you in your travels through this immense wilderness. For forty years now, God, your God, has been right here with you. You haven't lacked one thing.

DEUTERONOMY 2:7 MSG

God always blesses those who are kind to the poor and helpless. They're the first ones God helps when they find themselves in any trouble.

PSALM 41:1 TPT

The blessing of the LORD makes a person rich, and he adds no sorrow with it.

PROVERBS 10:22 NLT

Blessed is the one who reads aloud the words of this prophecy, and blessed are those who hear it and take to heart what is written in it, because the time is near.

REVELATION 1:3 NIV

CALLING

Some occupations aren't for everyone, for they require someone who responds to the job because of their calling. It has to be something you are deeply and truly convicted to pursue, something more than a career, a paycheck, or retirement. We often relate the word *calling* in the church to ecclesiastical pursuits as pastors, evangelists, teachers, or the like. But this is not the only case. Being a first responder in any capacity is a calling. It is a calling to be a servant. Using your natural gifts and skills developed over your career to serve each other, your community, and God is not a mundane job. It's a divine calling. It doesn't mean that you are promised a comfortable life. It means you are in the right place, and he will empower and equip you to do the work for which he purposed you.

Heavenly Father, I answered your call on my life to serve as a first responder. I do not take this call lightly. Guide my hands and feet, grant me wisdom, empower me with discernment, and give me the peace that surpasses all understanding. Amen.

How is serving as a first responder
helping you fulfill God's calling on your life?

The LORD said to me, "Do not say, 'I am too young.'
You must go to everyone I send you to
and say whatever I command you."

JEREMIAH 1:7 NIV

Jesus called out to them, "Come, follow me,
and I will show you how to fish for people!"

MARK 1:17 NLT

Jesus repeated his greeting, "Peace to you!"
And he told them, "Just as the Father has sent me,
I'm now sending you."

JOHN 20:21 TPT

A spiritual gift is given to each of us
so we can help each other.

1 CORINTHIANS 12:7 NLT

Samuel took a flask of olive oil and poured it on Saul's
head and kissed him, saying, "Has not the LORD anointed
you ruler over his inheritance?"

1 SAMUEL 10:1 NIV

CARE

For some of us, it is hard to believe that God cares about the most miniscule parts of our lives. But God is the Creator of the universe. He created everything we can see and many things still unknown to humankind. And since this is fact, all things, from his perspective, are small. But that doesn't mean they are not near to his heart. We see the issues of this world through the eyes of humanity, and often we fail to see them through the lens of the Creator of everything in existence. Care is a choice. It is motivated by love and a demonstration of kindness to others. If we are to be good stewards of the life we've been given, it requires us to not only learn to accept and receive care, but to also show care to others in their times of need. Does God care? Yes, he does. It's time we show the world that his people care about them, wherever they may be, whatever they may be walking through. Handle life with care!

Heavenly Father, you've shown great care in creating humanity, even the small details, like the number of hairs on our heads. Teach me to live in a way that shows your spirit lives in me, through the way I care for others. Amen.

Can you list three practical ways God cares for you daily as you serve your community?

The faithful lovers of God will inherit the earth and enjoy every promise of God's care, dwelling in peace forever.

PSALM 37:29 TPT

I will be your God throughout your lifetime—until your hair is white with age. I made you, and I will care for you. I will carry you along and save you.

ISAIAH 46:4 NLT

The LORD is good, a refuge in times of trouble. He cares for those who trust in him.

NAHUM 1:7 NIV

Look at the lilies and how they grow. They don't work or make their clothing, yet Solomon in all his glory was not dressed as beautifully as they are. And if God cares so wonderfully for flowers that are here today and thrown into the fire tomorrow, he will certainly care for you. Why do you have so little faith?

LUKE 12:27–28 NLT

CHOSEN

God didn't call animals to fulfill the law. No, he sent his Son, his only Son, Jesus, as the perfect lamb of God, to fulfill the old law. He sent him in the form of a man. From the foundations of the world, God chose you as an adopted son or daughter of his royal lineage. It's your choice whether you accept or reject that offer. It's not one to take lightly, for it comes with some serious responsibility. But knowing he has made available a way to eternal life with him gives us tremendous peace. We are chosen not just for salvation if we accept it and receive it but also for a life of being overcomers and conquerors of this world. There are many doctrines on this topic, but the essential truth is that God said you and I are worth sending his best, his Son Jesus, to redeem us, if we would only choose to accept it and live with the power of his spirit in us. You've been chosen. Who will you choose?

Heavenly Father, thank you for choosing me. Today, I want to respond to your demonstration of love to me by daily surrendering myself as a living sacrifice. My choice to follow you is a direct response of your love influencing my life. Amen.

How can your relationship with God
affect your choices in life?

For you are a people holy to the LORD your God.
The LORD your God has chosen you to be a people
for his treasured possession, out of all the peoples
who are on the face of the earth.

DEUTERONOMY 7:6 ESV

Be careful now, for the LORD has chosen you to build a
house for the sanctuary; be strong and do it.

1 CHRONICLES 28:10 ESV

Even before he made the world, God loved us and chose
us in Christ to be holy and without fault in his eyes.

EPHESIANS 1:4 NLT

Listen, my beloved brethren: Has God not chosen the
poor of this world to be rich in faith and heirs of the
kingdom which He promised to those who love Him?

JAMES 2:5 NKJV

You are a chosen people, a royal priesthood, a holy
nation, God's special possession, that you may declare
the praises of him who called you out of darkness into his
wonderful light.

1 PETER 2:9 NIV

COMFORT

When we are in a pit of despair, a place of grieving or distress, it is common to push others away. In hindsight, we can usually see where the power of God has comforted us, where he alleviated the pain, where he gave us freedom from negative, painful emotions. But while we're in those places, it's often hard to see the great Comforter at work. For one, while it is a natural tendency to want to push others away and isolate, know this is exactly what the enemy wants you to do. It's playing into his hand when we do this. Isolation can be good for a short period of time, but this is not the place where you will find healing. Look at the example of David in the book of Psalms. There were many times when he was in a place that seemed hopeless, but staying there was not an option. The comforting presence of God may not change your circumstances, but he will change your perspective, calm your emotions, and ease the pain you feel, if you will only invite him to do so and then allow him to do the work only he can do.

Heavenly Father, today, in the midst of a life that is often filled with pain and difficult circumstances, I welcome your presence. I'm not asking you to change the circumstances. I am only asking you to provide me with your presence that comforts me through it all. Amen.

In hindsight, can you see how God has comforted
you through hardships in your life?

Even though I walk through the darkest valley,
I will fear no evil, for you are with me;
your rod and your staff, they comfort me.

PSALM 23:4 NIV

As a mother comforts her son, so I will comfort you,
and you will be comforted in Jerusalem.

ISAIAH 66:13 HCSB

Young women will dance and be glad, young men
and old as well. I will turn their mourning into gladness;
I will give them comfort and joy instead of sorrow.

JEREMIAH 31:13 NIV

Praise the God and Father of our Lord Jesus Christ,
the Father of mercies and the God of all comfort.

2 CORINTHIANS 1:3 HCSB

COMPANIONSHIP

It is possible to be in a room with other people and still feel lonely. In fact, you can be in a relationship and feel lonely. God said in Genesis 2 that it was not good for man to be alone, so he created woman to be his companion and helper. There may come a time when the company of others leaves you feeling lonely, and when it does, it's a reminder that the void of companionship cannot be filled by a relationship with another human being but only with Jesus. When he is Lord of your life, you are never alone, and companionship with others is aligned properly. Maybe you've even been told that God was with you when you felt alone, and it rubbed you the wrong way. You may have thought, *That sounds great, but I don't feel God with me*. This is normal, but when we call out and draw near to him, he responds. Through Jesus, we have companionship with God, and through daily fellowship with him, we are empowered for healthy relationships in our lives. You are never alone when God is in you.

Heavenly Father, help me to always recognize your presence in my life, that your companionship with me is more important than anything else. I know I am never alone with you in my life.

How does daily fellowship with God make you a better companion in other relationships?

The LORD God said, "It is not good for the man to be alone. I will make a helper who is just right for him."
GENESIS 2:18 NLT

When the angel of the Lord appeared to Gideon, he said, "The LORD is with you, mighty warrior."
JUDGES 6:12 NIV

I know the LORD is always with me.
I will not be shaken, for he is right beside me.
PSALM 16:8 NLT

Teach these new disciples to obey all the commands I have given you. And be sure of this: I am with you always, even to the end of the age.
MATTHEW 28:20 NLT

Jesus answered and said to him, "If anyone loves Me, he will keep My word; and My Father will love him, and We will come to him and make Our home with him."
JOHN 14:23 NKJV

COMPASSION

We cannot demonstrate compassion for others until we have experienced this characteristic of God. To be compassionate people, having known both God's grace and compassion in our own experiences, we can then steward this gift from God. Think of times when you made mistakes on the job or sinned against God and others. How often has God demonstrated pity on you and me for our behaviors and the times of great trials? He is not a God who would ignore his people in times of distress. In our sin, before the foundation of the world, he demonstrated compassion to humanity when he sent his Son, Jesus, to pay the ultimate price once and for all. Having been the benefactors of such lovingkindness, we are now required to be good stewards of this gift for other people in our lives.

Heavenly Father, when I begin to be heavy handed with others, remind me of the compassion you have shown me, and help me remain compassionate in my service to your kingdom in this world. Amen.

How can you be a good steward of the gift of compassion with those you encounter today?

The LORD will indeed vindicate His people and have compassion on His servants when He sees that their strength is gone and no one is left—slave or free.

DEUTERONOMY 32:36 HCSB

The LORD is compassionate and gracious,
slow to anger, abounding in love.

PSALM 103:8 NIV

Because of our God's merciful compassion, the Dawn from on high will visit us to shine on those who live in darkness and the shadow of death, to guide our feet into the way of peace.

LUKE 1:78–79 HCSB

Show mercy and compassion for others,
just as your heavenly Father overflows
with mercy and compassion for all.

LUKE 6:36 TPT

As you know, we count as blessed those who have persevered. You have heard of Job's perseverance and have seen what the Lord finally brought about. The Lord is full of compassion and mercy.

JAMES 5:11 NIV

CONDEMNATION

In the context of biblical studies, *condemnation* is a term used to describe the punishment for sin. Think about it like this. If someone violates the law, they face investigations, arrest, trial, and if found guilty, a judgment is issued. For serious violent crimes, a court may sentence them to life in prison or condemn them to death. That is our sentence without Jesus in the equation: death. But because of Jesus, there is no longer condemnation but life everlasting. If we accept his sacrifice as payment for our sins, we acknowledge he was the substitute for what we should have experienced. Yes, there are earthly consequences for our sins, but if we accept him, and if we allow his love to change our hearts, then we will only die once. We live eternally. Today, embrace the truth of who Jesus is and what he has done for us, and allow the power of his love to affect your thoughts, words, and behavior. Eternal life is the reward for those who do this.

Heavenly Father, thank you for eternal life and for the reminder that there is no longer condemnation as I accept the truth of your Word in my heart. Amen.

How does the truth of God's Word set you free?

There is no longer any condemnation for those who
believe in him, but the unbeliever already lives under
condemnation because they do not believe in the name
of God's beloved Son.

JOHN 3:18 TPT

I speak to you an eternal truth: if you embrace my message
and believe in the One who sent me, you will never face
condemnation, for in me, you have already passed from
the realm of death into the realm of eternal life!

JOHN 5:24 TPT

There is no condemnation for those
who belong to Christ Jesus.

ROMANS 8:1 NLT

Our actions will show that we belong to the truth,
so we will be confident when we stand before God.
Even if we feel guilty, God is greater than our feelings,
and he knows everything.

1 JOHN 3:19–20 NLT

CONFIDENCE

Most folks don't know how to handle the personalities of "sheepdogs." Here's the truth: sheepdogs walk with confidence that most people would pay a lifetime salary to possess. Sure, this is partly due to the training, experience, and knowledge they have gained on the job, but it goes deeper. That's the spirit of a sheepdog, which is any first responder. Without the power of God in our lives, this confidence is short lived. Before you head into duty, know that God is the source of all you need. You are equipped with righteous confidence to address the enemies you will face in the spiritual battle and the enemies in this world. Being confident does not mean you are arrogant, and "religious" folk will accuse you of such because they are not familiar with godly confidence. Walk in the power you have been given, never lower your head, and remember whose you are.

Heavenly Father, thank you for the confidence found in your presence, through your Word, and in prayer. Today, I walk in that confidence, not only for the battles of this life but also in the eternal life I have been given through Jesus.

How do you explain the difference between
confidence and pride?

The LORD turned to him and said,
"Go with the strength you have,
and rescue Israel from the Midianites.
I am sending you!"

JUDGES 6:14 NLT

They are confident and fearless
and can face their foes triumphantly.

PSALM 112:8 NLT

Dear brothers and sisters, we can boldly enter heaven's
Most Holy Place because of the blood of Jesus. By his
death, Jesus opened a new and life-giving way through
the curtain into the Most Holy Place.

HEBREWS 10:19–20 NLT

CONTENTMENT

When we die, we will leave behind all the things in life that we experience with our physical senses. Nothing we can obtain in our efforts will go with us into eternity. When we live life with this eternal perspective, we are closer to living a life of contentment, which leads to great freedom. Living life contently doesn't mean we should do so without goals or ambitions or that we should not desire material things. However, it does mean we should obtain those things with eternity at the forefront of our motives. One of the things we can do to discover this place in life is to keep our hearts centered on God, not being greedy or materialistic, but by being generous. Once contentment becomes a way of life for you, all the striving in the world takes a back seat to eternal priorities, and gratitude becomes a daily habit. Living content is living well.

Heavenly Father, you know the desires of my heart, and you know my motives. Help me keep these things in check so they honor you. Teach me contentment so I can live with gratitude. Amen.

How can contentment help you grow closer to God?

You're blessed when you're content with just who you are—
no more, no less. That's the moment you find yourselves
proud owners of everything that can't be bought.

MATTHEW 5:5 MSG

Godliness with contentment is great gain. For we
brought nothing into this world, and it is certain we can
carry nothing out. And having food and clothing, with
these we shall be content.

1 TIMOTHY 6:6–8 NKJV

Don't be obsessed with money but live content with what
you have, for you always have God's presence. For hasn't
he promised you, "I will never leave you alone, never!
And I will not loosen my grip on your life!"

HEBREWS 13:5 TPT

COURAGE

Courage is contagious. It could be courage that drives you to do something stupid, as many of us did as children, or it could be courage that drives us to change the world. These are two extremes, but the reality is that all it takes is one person who is willing to overcome the opposition to the message of truth and righteousness to crush evil in this world. How are courageous men and women created? Through examples of past generations of heroes who remained undeterred in the face of fear. Heroes know the power of God in them is greater than the evil in this world, and they walk in confidence found in Christ. It's not a superpower, but it is something we must develop and nurture. There is no place in the kingdom of God for cowards. Only the courageous inherit it.

Heavenly Father, I walk with the power of your spirit, knowing that because of you, I am empowered to be courageous in my endeavors to share your good news with others. Amen.

How does courage empower you to fulfill God's purpose for your life?

Look! He has placed the land in front of you. Go and occupy it as the LORD, the God of your ancestors, has promised you. Don't be afraid! Don't be discouraged!

DEUTERONOMY 1:21 NLT

He said: "Listen, King Jehoshaphat and all who live in Judah and Jerusalem! This is what the LORD says to you: 'Do not be afraid or discouraged because of this vast army. For the battle is not yours, but God's.'"

2 CHRONICLES 20:15 NIV

Be strong and courageous and do it. Do not be afraid and do not be dismayed, for the LORD God, even my God, is with you. He will not leave you or forsake you, until all the work for the service of the house of the LORD is finished.

1 CHRONICLES 28:20 ESV

Don't lose your bold, courageous faith, for you are destined for a great reward!

HEBREWS 10:35 TPT

COVENANT

As Americans, we think often in terms of contracts, terms and conditions, and legal boundaries. But this was not the case when fifty-six men signed the Declaration of Independence over two hundred years ago. The most popular secular covenant, a spiritual agreement, a higher form of agreement than a contract, is the Declaration of Independence. The last line reads: "And for the support of this Declaration, with a firm reliance on the protection of divine Providence, we mutually pledge to each other our Lives, our Fortunes and our sacred Honor." Many Americans have lost the will to fight for each other and mutually pledge their lives, fortunes, and honor to each other across the aisles. Let our lives be the markers of freedom, mercy, and justice. Let our lives honor our fore-fathers' sacrifices and epitomize liberty, as one nation under God, for ages to come.

Heavenly Father, thank you for the new covenant found through the sacrifice of your Son, Jesus. I walk in the freedom made possible by your life. Amen.

How does a covenant, as opposed to a contract,
improve the relationship between two parties?

Behold, I am making a covenant. Before all your people
I will do marvels, such as have not been created in all
the earth or in any nation. And all the people among
whom you are shall see the work of the LORD, for it is an
awesome thing that I will do with you.

EXODUS 34:10 ESV

If you pay attention to these laws and are careful to follow
them, then the LORD your God will keep his covenant of
love with you, as he swore to your ancestors.

DEUTERONOMY 7:12 NIV

Jesus has now obtained a superior ministry, and to that
degree He is the mediator of a better covenant, which has
been legally enacted on better promises.

HEBREWS 8:6 HCSB

I will make a covenant of peace with them;
it will be an everlasting covenant.
I will establish them and increase their numbers,
and I will put my sanctuary among them forever.

EZEKIEL 37:26 NIV

DEATH

The average American will live about seventy-eight years or 28,470 days.[2] What will you do this day? Death is unavoidable, but it is seldom easily explained in moments of grief. Few, if any, words can offer comfort to those who have lost a loved one. However, it is comforting to know that Jesus defeated death, and while we will die a natural death, leaving this physical body behind, there is eternal life in his presence if we accept him as Lord and Savior. When we are absent from this body, we are present with God in eternity. Think about that. God's presence is with us through this life on earth, and as his children, we are in his presence forever. In a grieving time, the most powerful gift we can give those who grieve is being present. Words are often unnecessary. We will not bypass physical death, but we can avoid spiritual death by accepting Christ as our Savior.

Heavenly Father, in life and death, you comfort me. You sustain me through all things, and you give me peace through all things. Help me to live a life worthy of the love you've shown me so I can have eternal life with you. Amen.

---

2   "Faststats: Life expectancy," National Center for Health Statistics, Center for Disease Control and Prevention, March 17, 2017, https://www.cdc.gov.

How does the reality of death impact your decisions today?

When one of God's holy lovers dies,
it is costly to the LORD,
touching his heart.

PSALM 116:15 TPT

Blessed are those who die in the LORD from now on. Yes,
says the Spirit, they are blessed indeed, for they will rest
from their hard work; for their good deeds follow them!

REVELATION 14:13 NLT

I speak to you this eternal truth: whoever cherishes my
words and keeps them will never experience death.

JOHN 8:51 TPT

For me, living is Christ and dying is gain.

PHILIPPIANS 1:21 HCSB

The wicked are crushed by every calamity, but the lovers
of God find a strong hope even in the time of death.

PROVERBS 14:32 TPT

DEFENSE

A common saying I recall from growing up in church is, "If the devil ain't attacking you, you ain't living right." God did not provide us with spiritual armor for our pleasure and enjoyment. He equipped us with it for battle. And battles are not without the enemy's attacks. We do not base our defense strategy on physical weapons alone. Instead, we discover it in times of prayer and fasting. The Holy Spirit is our defense against the enemy's spiritual attacks. He equips us, and he sustains us. There are times when the most effective protection is obeying his command to "be still" (Psalm 46:10 ESV). God's commandments aren't *only* to address sinful behavior. They are also to protect us from the evil one. When we walk in the truth of God's Word and follow him, we will face many battles, but with his Word, through prayer, and depending on his Spirit, we can overcome and be victorious. Our defense is the presence of God. Spend time in his presence and prepare for battle.

Heavenly Father, go before me in the assignments I have been given in life. As I seek you and study your Word, equip me with the spiritual armor I need to be victorious. You are my defense. Amen.

How does spiritual defense strategy differ from physical defense strategy?

The LORD is my revelation-light to guide me along the way; he's the source of my salvation to defend me every day. I fear no one! I'll never turn back and run from you, LORD; surround and protect me.

PSALM 27:1 TPT

God sends angels with special orders to protect you wherever you go, defending you from all harm.

PSALM 91:11 TPT

Don't rob the poor just because you can, or exploit the needy in court. For the LORD is their defender. He will ruin anyone who ruins them.

PROVERBS 22:22–23 NLT

The LORD is with me like a violent warrior. Therefore, my persecutors will stumble and not prevail. Since they have not succeeded, they will be utterly shamed, an everlasting humiliation that will never be forgotten.

JEREMIAH 20:11 HCSB

DELIVERANCE

The term *deliverance* in the Bible is often synonymous with the casting out of demons. While that is one usage of the word, it is not the only one. In the Bible, deliverance can be the act of God removing his people from evil influence or oppression, or it could be an individual or people being delivered into the hands of someone for judgment. Deliverance isn't the sole assignment of vocational ministers. In fact, it is our job as members of the body of Christ. As first responders, we must walk in the commandments of Jesus and not only cast out demons and help others find deliverance from addiction, abuse, and other evil, but those in law enforcement must also bring judgment to those who violate the law. May your focus be on loving others so well and mirroring the love of God that they want to run to him and abandon all the things of this world that hold them down.

Heavenly Father, empower me to fulfill my assignment in this world, direct my steps, grant me wisdom and discernment, and protect me from the evil one. May my life reflect your love for others. Amen.

How can your life be a beacon of hope for those
who need deliverance?

The Lord is my rock,
my fortress and my deliverer.

2 Samuel 22:2 NIV

The Lord your God you shall fear; and He will deliver you
from the hand of all your enemies.

2 Kings 17:39 NKJV

He is my faithful love and my fortress, my stronghold
and my deliverer. He is my shield, and I take refuge in
Him; He subdues my people under me.

Psalm 144:2 HCSB

Everyone who calls on the name of the Lord will be
saved; for on Mount Zion and in Jerusalem there will
be deliverance, as the Lord has said, even among the
survivors whom the Lord calls.

Joel 2:32 NIV

He has delivered us from such a terrible death, and He
will deliver us. We have put our hope in Him that He will
deliver us again.

2 Corinthians 1:10 HCSB

DEPRESSION

I am not writing this from the perspective of a doctor or a counselor but as a brother in Christ. There are not only mental and physical causes for depression, but there are also spiritual components that cause this issue in our lives. In my own experience, I remember a time in my life when depression felt like an anchor keeping me in bed. I lost all desire to do the things I used to enjoy, and my appetite was wildly off-kilter. It's a unique challenge, and sometimes medication is beneficial. The day I understood that my depression went beyond a physical and mental illness and was also rooted in spiritual causes, I learned how to address the source. I began to ask God to restore the joy of my salvation, and instead of seeking hope in the things of this world, I sought him as my hope. When our focus is on Jesus, we can find our way out of the pit of despair. It is not a sin to be in this place, but it is a sin to magnify it higher than the name of Jesus in your life. He is bigger than the greatest battle you will ever face.

Heavenly Father, teach me to encourage myself in you. When I lose my focus, help me to remember your love for me and the source of my hope and joy. Amen.

How can hope in Christ help you dig out of a place of despair?

God's Message: "I'll turn things around for Jacob. I'll compassionately come in and rebuild homes. The town will be rebuilt on its old foundations; the mansions will be splendid again. Thanksgivings will pour out of the windows; laughter will spill through the doors. Things will get better and better. Depression days are over. They'll thrive, they'll flourish. The days of contempt will be over."

JEREMIAH 30:19 MSG

Fear no more, Jacob, dear servant. Don't despair, Israel. Look up! I'll save you out of faraway places, I'll bring your children back from exile. Jacob will come back and find life good, safe and secure.

JEREMIAH 30:10 MSG

We are pressed on every side by troubles, but we are not crushed. We are perplexed, but not driven to despair.

2 CORINTHIANS 4:8 NLT

DISCIPLESHIP

Following Jesus is more than reading a few Scripture verses and saying a prayer before your next meal. It requires growth through discipleship, setting the life of Jesus as your model, and demonstrating his principles through the way you live. This life is more than preaching sermons within the four walls of a church building. God's Word commands us to go out and make disciples for Christ, which is only possible if we submit to his way and follow him. Think about it like this: If you are a firearms instructor, how would you feel if someone else received a more advanced level of firearms instructor training before completing the lessons you completed? Or if someone else with no other training came into your profession at a higher rank? So it is with discipleship. We first must be disciples before we can disciple others. Follow the pattern laid out by Jesus and the twelve disciples in the New Testament, and let's come together and fulfill this great commandment of Jesus.

Heavenly Father, keep my heart soft and tender toward you, and stir daily a hunger in my soul for the things of your kingdom. As I follow you, let me lead others to your Son, Jesus. Amen.

How does discipleship empower you as a follower of Christ?

Jesus said to his disciples, "If any of you wants to be my follower, you must give up your own way, take up your cross, and follow me."

MATTHEW 16:24 NLT

If you tenderly care for this little child on my behalf, you are tenderly caring for me. And if you care for me, you are honoring my Father who sent me. For the one who is least important in your eyes is actually the most important one of all.

LUKE 9:48 TPT

Let's not get tired of doing what is good. At just the right time we will reap a harvest of blessing if we don't give up.

GALATIANS 6:9 NLT

This is how we know who the children of God are and who the children of the devil are: Anyone who does not do what is right is not God's child, nor is anyone who does not love their brother and sister.

1 JOHN 3:10 NIV

DISCIPLINE

Once we surrender our hearts, minds, and lives to God, our desires do not govern our lives. Jesus said to pick up the cross, follow him. The governing authority of the kingdom of God is not the same as this world. In fact, it is quite the opposite. The first shall be last in God's kingdom, so if you want to be a leader, you must be a servant. Great warriors are men and women who will wash the feet of others. It is nothing like this world. It requires discipline, which means doing the "God" things even when it is not easy, is not popular, or does not benefit us directly at the moment. Disciplined followers of Christ do his will even when it is against our own wills. We must live our lives according to God's Word, the higher and ultimate standard of discipline. It's a higher standard, but it is one by which our lives will produce fruit for his kingdom for all eternity.

Heavenly Father, when I get physically and emotionally tired, give me the mindset and willpower to continue doing the things I know are right according to your Word, for this is the spiritual discipline I seek. Amen.

How can you use spiritual discipline in your life to produce fruit in other areas of your life?

My child, when the Lord God speaks to you, never take his words lightly, and never be upset when he corrects you. For the Father's discipline comes only from his passionate love and pleasure for you. Even when it seems like his correction is harsh, it's still better than any father on earth gives to his child.

PROVERBS 3:11–12 TPT

Our earthly fathers disciplined us for a few years, doing the best they knew how. But God's discipline is always good for us, so that we might share in his holiness. No discipline is enjoyable while it is happening—it's painful! But afterward there will be a peaceful harvest of right living for those who are trained in this way.

HEBREWS 12:10–11 NLT

I correct and discipline everyone I love. So be diligent and turn from your indifference.

REVELATION 3:19 NLT

DISOBEDIENCE

Willfully violating God's commandments is one of the most dangerous things we do in life, especially since we know right from wrong. Often we still choose to disobey God even though we know the difference between right and wrong. There was a time in life when ignorance was a valid excuse, likely between the ages of one and three. Nobody expects infants and toddlers to know the difference between right or wrong, but as an adult and as a first responder, you know the difference. Disobedience to God's love means we do not live in a way that is a proper response to the love he has shown us. We know stealing, lying, cheating, and murder are wrong, but Jesus gave a higher standard when he said if these things are in our hearts, we have sinned. We should see every day as an opportunity to change negative behaviors and live a life of obedience that honors God. Every day is a new opportunity for our lives to reflect the love he's shown us by loving others.

Heavenly Father, thank you for your mercy, which is new every morning. I am thankful for your forgiveness. Never let me take for granted the amazing grace you have shown me. Amen.

How does God's Word help equip you to live a life obedient to him?

If you have a change of heart, refuse to listen obediently, and willfully go off to serve and worship other gods, you will most certainly die. You won't last long in the land that you are crossing the Jordan to enter and possess.

DEUTERONOMY 30:17–18 MSG

This is what God says: "Why do you disobey the LORD's commands? You will not prosper. Because you have forsaken the LORD, he has forsaken you."

2 CHRONICLES 24:20 NIV

The face of the LORD is set against those who do what is evil, to erase all memory of them from the earth.

PSALM 34:16 HCSB

The Lord your God will raise up a prophet from among you who is like me. Listen to him and follow everything he tells you. Every person who disobeys that prophet will be cut off and completely destroyed.

ACTS 3:22–23 TPT

ENEMIES

When we think of the state's enemies, we might think of a foreign power that wants to destroy our way of life. Maybe you can think back to school when someone bullied you or someone you knew. That person may have seemed like an enemy to you. However, there are times when it is not so easy to identify our enemies. Such is the case with the enemy of our souls and, ultimately, the enemy of God. The enemy of God is the natural behavior of man: sin. Sin is a product of hell, formulated for humanity, created specifically for our destruction. While Satan is the chief enemy of God, it is sin that is the enemy of humanity and God. Yes, there will be enemies in this life, enemies who are human beings, but they are merely vehicles of obedience that the kingdom of darkness uses to oppose your mission of being the salt and light of the earth for God's kingdom. Identify the enemy, which is sin, and share the solution, which is Jesus. Enemies will always exist in this life, but so does the victorious King of Glory.

Heavenly Father, I know the enemy of my soul is sin, the kingdom of darkness, and people who are operatives for Satan. I know you are for me now and always. I pray for my enemies, and I give them to you. Amen.

If hell can use people to be enemies of God and his people, how can you allow God to use you to reach others for Christ?

The LORD your God will put all these curses on your enemies who hate and persecute you.

DEUTERONOMY 30:7 HCSB

Your hand will find all Your enemies; Your right hand will find those who hate You. You shall make them as a fiery oven in the time of Your anger; The LORD shall swallow them up in His wrath, And the fire shall devour them.

PSALM 21:8–9 NKJV

He will crush every enemy, shattering their strength. He will make heads roll for they refuse to repent of their stubborn, sinful ways.

PSALM 68:21 TPT

I will force those who belong to Satan's synagogue—those liars who say they are Jews but are not—to come and bow down at your feet. They will acknowledge that you are the ones I love.

REVELATION 3:9 NLT

ETERNAL LIFE

If we build our entire life around what we can gain materially or through careers, our joy will be limited, our peace will be easily disturbed, and our minds will be cluttered and clouded. When we base our perspective of life on eternity, our behavior will align properly. Eternal life is the ultimate reward for those who surrender their hearts and lives to Jesus. Eternal life is not a fairytale that exists merely in the pages of an ancient book. It is a reality for those who will walk in God's promises, our Creator, the Alpha and Omega. If you want to live for all eternity in God's presence, it begins with repentance, surrendering to God, and walking in his commandments. Live a life that focuses on storing up riches for eternity through kingdom-minded living. Inviting Jesus into our hearts to be our Savior and Lord is the only way to receive eternal life. To receive eternal life, we must begin by surrendering our lives to him daily and fellowshipping with him in prayer and Bible study.

Heavenly Father, thank you for the gift of eternal life. You have blessed me with so many perfect gifts, but this one is better than them all. I receive it now and choose to surrender my heart, mind, and life to you today and every day. Amen.

How does living life with eternal perspective shift your decisions in this life?

I give them eternal life, and they will never perish. No one can snatch them away from me, for my Father has given them to me, and he is more powerful than anyone else. No one can snatch them from the Father's hand.

JOHN 10:28–29 NLT

Now that you have been set free from sin and have become slaves of God, the benefit you reap leads to holiness, and the result is eternal life. For the wages of sin is death, but the gift of God is eternal life in Christ Jesus our Lord.

ROMANS 6:22–23 NIV

Don't you realize that in a race everyone runs, but only one person gets the prize? So run to win! All athletes are disciplined in their training. They do it to win a prize that will fade away, but we do it for an eternal prize.

1 CORINTHIANS 9:24–25 NLT

You, dear friends, must build each other up in your most holy faith, pray in the power of the Holy Spirit, and await the mercy of our Lord Jesus Christ, who will bring you eternal life. In this way, you will keep yourselves safe in God's love.

JUDE 20–21 NLT

EVIL

During your service as a responder, you will look into the face of evil. You may have already witnessed evil at work, or you will most assuredly do so in your future. What else can you call it when we see children murdered or abused and helpless innocents harmed in horrific ways. *This* is the face of evil, and you are a living shield of flesh and blood, standing between evil and the precious innocent lives of others. If you believe in a force of evil—and who can deny it—then you are doomed in your endeavors if you do not also believe in a superior force for good and apply that force for good in your daily life. Indeed, the presence of evil is solid proof of God and his holy forces of good. When the sun is eclipsed by the moon, we cannot bear to look directly at the sun, but the darkness of the eclipse proves the presence of light. So, too, does the darkness of evil prove the presence of good. The opposite of love is not hate; it is evil. Evil is the absence of love, just as darkness is the absence of light. And God *is* love! All love emanates from him. His love is infinite and beyond any earthly love that we can comprehend. Thus we respond to evil with confidence and with the most powerful force in the universe: God's love.

Heavenly Father, thank you for your love and for teaching me to confront evil with love. I know you love me. Help me to love you, to love others, and to tell others about your great love. Amen.

How do you differentiate between hate and evil?

Hate evil, and love good,
and establish justice in the gate.

AMOS 5:15 ESV

The fear of the LORD is hatred of evil. Pride and arrogance
and the way of evil and perverted speech I hate.

PROVERBS 8:13 ESV

Even though I walk through the valley of the shadow of
death, I will fear no evil, for you are with me; your rod
and your staff, they comfort me.

PSALM 23:4 ESV

We do not wrestle against flesh and blood, but against the
rulers, against the authorities, against the cosmic powers
over this present darkness, against the spiritual forces of
evil in the heavenly places.

EPHESIANS 6:12 ESV

Do not be overcome by evil,
but overcome evil with good.

ROMANS 12:21 ESV

FAIRNESS

The cry for fair treatment and justice is, in most cases, a universal desire by all humanity. When we speak of fairness in a religious context, we can agree that there are times when it does not seem God is fair, and life often isn't. At times, even justice seems unfair. Sometimes, God favors some people, but it is only deemed unfair by those who are not beneficiaries of that favor. So what is fairness? It is the application of God's grace across every life who will receive it. It is the application of the perfect sacrifice of his Son, Jesus, for all who will accept it. Fairness isn't addressed adequately or daily in the context of this life, but when we see it through the lens of eternity or through God's eyes, we understand just how perfect it is. It is an absolute certainty that God wants fairness in our lives, probably even more than we desire it.

Heavenly Father, thank you for teaching me what fairness means and what it looks like in this life. I know you are fair to me and desire it in my life. Help me to treat others with fairness. Amen.

How do you differentiate between fairness and justice?

Do you know what I want?
I want justice—oceans of it.
I want fairness—rivers of it.
That's what I want.
That's all I want.

AMOS 5:24 MSG

Peter said, "Now I know for certain that God doesn't show favoritism with people but treats everyone on the same basis. It makes no difference what race of people one belongs to. If they show deep reverence for God, and are committed to doing what's right, they are acceptable before him."

ACTS 10:34–35 TPT

Masters, treat your slaves the same way, without threatening them, because you know that both their Master and yours is in heaven, and there is no favoritism with Him.

EPHESIANS 6:9 HCSB

FAITH

Faith is something we speak of often in church. We sing about it in various hymns and songs and read about it in books. It is a beautiful and powerful gift. Each person possesses a measure of faith, but God has blessed some with a *gift* of faith. Dear friends, faith isn't proven when things are going well. It is in these times when faith is in training. When you have complete assurance in the things of this world that everything is going to unfold as you see it, that's not faith. When you are standing by a loved one in critical care, when you are present to comfort a grieving loved one, or when you endure terrible trials in your life, that is where faith is needed most. When you don't know what to do next, rely on your faith. When you are unsure of what tomorrow holds, rely on your faith in the one who sustains today, has forgiven yesterday, and holds tomorrow firmly in his hands.

Heavenly Father, when my faith is not strong, strengthen me. For you are my portion, and I rely on you. Amen.

How can faith in God help you through traumatic events in life?

I assure you: If you have faith the size of a mustard seed, you will tell this mountain, "Move from here to there," and it will move. Nothing will be impossible for you.

MATTHEW 17:20 HCSB

Because of our faith, Christ has brought us into this place of undeserved privilege where we now stand, and we confidently and joyfully look forward to sharing God's glory.

ROMANS 5:2 NLT

It is by grace you have been saved, through faith— and this is not from yourselves, it is the gift of God.

EPHESIANS 2:8 NIV

Without faith it is impossible to please God, because anyone who comes to him must believe that he exists and that he rewards those who earnestly seek him.

HEBREWS 11:6 NIV

Faith by itself isn't enough. Unless it produces good deeds, it is dead and useless.

JAMES 2:17 NLT

FAMILY

As first responders, you've heard fellow public servants refer to each other as "brother" or "sister." This designation isn't tossed around carelessly, and it isn't taken lightly. It's a title that is earned. Family isn't limited to your siblings, your parents, and those others who share your same last name. Your family includes those who stick by you when you are at your absolute worst, when you have nothing to offer them, and when you are most unlovable. As first responders, you have a family who is willing to die for strangers, and they are prepared to die for you. As a follower of Christ, you are part of a global family with one mission: to love God and love others. It's a bond unlike any other. When we see a brother or sister in Christ suffering, we should find a way to intervene and serve them. Family is an inseparable bond. One that isn't limited to DNA. If you are willing to serve with and die for someone and love them unconditionally through their worst, you are family.

Heavenly Father, thank you for my family, and thank you for having me in your family. Help me to leave a legacy of love and one that honors your great name. Amen.

How can family strengthen you
for the battles you will face?

Look up into the sky and count the stars if you can.
That's how many descendants you will have!

GENESIS 15:5 NLT

"Cursed be anyone who dishonors his father or his
mother." And all the people shall say, "Amen."

DEUTERONOMY 27:16 ESV

Your family and your kingdom are permanently secured.
I'm keeping my eye on them! And your royal throne will
always be there, rock solid.

2 SAMUEL 7:16 MSG

Your wife will be like a fruitful grapevine, flourishing
within your home. Your children will be like vigorous
young olive trees as they sit around your table. That is the
LORD's blessing for those who fear him.

PSALM 128:3–4 NLT

How wonderful, how beautiful,
when brothers and sisters get along!

PSALM 133:1 MSG

FEAR

Fear is a powerful emotion that first responders deal with every day. It can be an empowering force that drives us through moments of danger or a source of self-preservation. Whatever the circumstances, when it is paired with discernment, we can thrive in conflict. But fear can also be one of the things that keep us from reaching our full potential in this life, and it can keep us from walking in the fullness of what God created us to be. There's no eliminating fear, only overcoming it, only knowing how to navigate it. Don't ignore its signs, rather know when it is time to regroup and reapproach. Never allow fear to paralyze you and keep you from doing what God has called you to do. God has not given us a spirit of fear. Rather, he has given us a sound mind and power to overcome fear. How will you respond to fear today?

Heavenly Father, I know there are different types of fear, and my fear of you is not one of terror, rather one of reverence. Stir in me the power and sound mind to overcome the fear rooted in the enemy that aims to debilitate me. Amen.

How can you distinguish between holy fear and evil fear?

Have I not commanded you? Be strong and of good courage; do not be afraid, nor be dismayed, for the LORD your God is with you wherever you go.

JOSHUA 1:9 NKJV

I lie down and sleep; I wake again, because the LORD sustains me. I will not fear though tens of thousands assail me on every side.

PSALM 3:5–6 NIV

Do not fear, for I am with you; do not be afraid, for I am your God.

ISAIAH 41:10 HCSB

Don't be afraid of those who want to kill your body; they cannot touch your soul. Fear only God, who can destroy both soul and body in hell.

MATTHEW 10:28 NLT

There is no fear in love. But perfect love drives out fear, because fear has to do with punishment. The one who fears is not made perfect in love.

1 JOHN 4:18 NIV

FORGIVENESS

Forgiveness can be an easy thing to extend when the offense is minor or not directed against you. But when you or someone you love has been severely hurt, either physically or emotionally, forgiveness can be much more challenging. Think about it like this: God has forgiven you, and if someone offends you, God expects you to forgive as he has forgiven. If you have hurt someone, you would desire forgiveness, but you also need to forgive yourself. It's a multidimensional need between all parties and God. There are times when forgiveness for another party is best expressed between you and God, consciously, in prayer, without approaching the other party or involving them. This doesn't mean they get off the hook, and it doesn't say you are no longer feeling the pain. It means you are no longer going to entertain the narrative of the circumstances, and you are not going to continue revisiting the details and what could have been. It's one of the healthiest things you can do to overcome an offense against you.

Heavenly Father, thank you for your mercy and forgiveness in my life. For every moment, your forgiveness is available to me. Give me the power and strength to forgive others and myself when offense occurs. Amen.

When someone hurts you, why does forgiveness
affect you (the forgiver) more than the offender?
What are the benefits of forgiveness?

He forgives your sins—every one.

PSALM 103:3 MSG

I have swept away your offenses like a cloud,
your sins like the morning mist.
Return to me, for I have redeemed you.

ISAIAH 44:22 NIV

When you are praying, first forgive anyone you are
holding a grudge against, so that your Father in heaven
will forgive your sins, too.

MARK 11:25 NLT

We have redemption, the forgiveness of sins, in Him.

COLOSSIANS 1:14 HCSB

If our sins have been forgiven and forgotten, why would
we ever need to offer another sacrifice for sin?

HEBREWS 10:18 TPT

FREEDOM

As Americans, we see freedom as a political issue and a way of life. Many men and women have given their lives for us to experience freedom from tyranny. We are free to worship, free to pursue happiness, and free to live lives governed by liberty and love. While this freedom is a way of life for Americans, it is not the greatest freedom. The greatest freedom we have is freedom from the power of sin and death through Jesus. That's a reason to celebrate! Jesus redeemed us, and he gave us power over sin, freedom from the power of sin, and freedom from death. We celebrate America's independence every year, but we should rise joyfully every new day and celebrate the freedom Jesus has provided. Every recipient of freedom in Jesus will be held accountable for how they respond to this new way of life. How will you respond?

Heavenly Father, thank you for freedom from the power of sin and for freedom found in you to live a life to the fullest. I know that where your presence is, there is freedom. Abide in me. Amen.

Knowing freedom exists where the presence of the Lord is, how can you be a better host of the Spirit of God in your life and experience victory in this life in preparation for eternity?

Everyone who believes in him is set free from sin and guilt—something the law of Moses had no power to do.

ACTS 13:39 TPT

When we died with Christ we were set free
from the power of sin.

ROMANS 6:7 NLT

The Lord is the Spirit,
and where the Spirit of the Lord is,
there is freedom.

2 CORINTHIANS 3:17 HCSB

You have died with Christ, and he has set you free from the spiritual powers of this world. So why do you keep on following the rules of the world?

COLOSSIANS 2:20 NLT

FULFILLMENT

In an age where personal development and improvement are hot selling topics, personal fulfillment is often a vital issue. When you work in a career where you do not feel fulfilled, many suggest you need to find another line of work. But when the Bible mentions fulfillment, it's not referring to personal development or self-satisfaction. Instead, it's referring to the fulfillment of God's promises, and Jesus fulfilled the law. When he came and willingly died for all sins, he completed the old covenant where animal sacrifices were required. Now we are required only to live a life of daily sacrifice to the Lord. Our fulfillment isn't found in careers, relationships, material things, or money. It's found in a relationship with Jesus alone! He fulfilled all that was required, and through him, all the promises of Scripture for those who follow him will be fulfilled.

Heavenly Father, thank you for keeping your promises, for always keeping your word. I know your promises will all be fulfilled in my life, and I will experience complete fulfillment when I walk in obedience to you. Amen.

How can you experience fulfillment in life
by clinging to the promises of God?

Remember the LORD your God. He is the one who
gives you power to be successful, in order to fulfill the
covenant he confirmed to your ancestors with an oath.

DEUTERONOMY 8:18 NLT

Not a single one of all the good promises the LORD
had given to the family of Israel was left unfulfilled;
everything he had spoken came true.

JOSHUA 21:45 NLT

You are the LORD who reigns over your never-ending
kingdom through all the ages of time and eternity!
You are faithful to fulfill every promise you've made.
You manifest yourself as kindness in all you do.

PSALM 145:13 TPT

"The days are coming," declares the LORD, "when I will
fulfill the good promise I made to the people of Israel
and Judah."

JEREMIAH 33:14 NIV

FUTURE

Before you can address your future, you must first address your past. If the redeeming love of God does not secure our pasts, we cannot discuss our futures. But when we surrender our lives to God and give him our sins, struggles, and past failures, we realize our future is full of hope, not harm, full of faith, not fear, and our long-term future is promising. Consider the price that Jesus paid to secure our futures. Every thought must be taken captive if not in line with Scripture, and every word must be spoken according to the authority we've been given in his Word. When our thoughts and words align with God's, we begin to make decisions and take actions that are not only biblical but also healthier and more productive. We are called to be *holy*, which means set apart and not like the world. The past is taken care of thanks to Jesus. Our futures are full of hope, so all we have to do is walk in the promises of his Word.

Heavenly Father, thank you for forgiving the sins of my past, for separating them as far as the east is from the west. I give you my past, my present, and trust you with my future. Amen.

Planning is critical and wise. How can you surrender your life to a sovereign God while planning for the future?

Watch the blameless and observe the upright, for the man of peace will have a future. But transgressors will all be eliminated; the future of the wicked will be destroyed.

PSALM 37:37–38 HCSB

Only I can tell you the future before it even happens.
Everything I plan will come to pass,
for I do whatever I wish.

ISAIAH 46:10 NLT

The day of the Lord will come as a thief in the night, in which the heavens will pass away with a great noise, and the elements will melt with fervent heat; both the earth and the works that are in it will be burned up.

2 PETER 3:10 NKJV

I'm on my way; I'll be there soon.
Keep a tight grip on what you have
so no one distracts you and steals your crown.

REVELATION 3:11 MSG

GENEROSITY

Often when we hear the word *generosity*, we think of giving financially, especially as it relates to benevolence. Too often, our generosity is limited to charity, offerings, and material donations to the church or those less fortunate. However, generosity isn't limited to finances or material things. The greatest gift is love. "Now these three remain: faith, hope, and love. But the greatest of these is love" (1 Corinthians 13:13 HCSB). We are blessed to be a blessing, and maybe you don't have an abundance of finances to give, but we all have love to offer. We can all speak a word of encouragement. As first responders, you give your best every day. You are a living example of generosity. There's no greater demonstration of love and generosity than someone who willingly puts his or her life in harm's way for others. Yes, be generous with your material things and even your finances. But be more generous with your love and time, especially when it comes to those you call family.

Heavenly Father, thank you for being generous with your love, mercy, and goodness in my life. You have taught me how to be generous. May my life be an example of generosity in all things. Amen.

How does generosity strengthen you as a child of God? Can you see his faithfulness as you are generous to others?

When you are generous to the poor,
you are enriched with blessings in return.
PROVERBS 22:9 TPT

Be wary of the shrewd advice that tells you how to get ahead in the world on your own. Giving, not getting, is the way. Generosity begets generosity. Stinginess impoverishes.
MARK 4:24–25 MSG

If you free your heart of greed, showing compassion and true generosity to the poor, you have more than clean hands; you will be clean within.
LUKE 11:41 TPT

In everything I did, I showed you that by this kind of hard work we must help the weak, remembering the words the Lord Jesus himself said: "It is more blessed to give than to receive."
ACTS 20:35 NIV

We will show mercy to the poor and not miss an opportunity to do acts of kindness for others, for these are the true sacrifices that delight God's heart.
HEBREWS 13:16 TPT

GOODNESS

According to one study,[3] up to 60% of the human body is water. We cannot exist without water in our bodies. When we speak of God and goodness, it is like talking of human beings and water. There is no good without God. It is the core of who he is. We see his goodness in everyday life, through his children's actions, when he turns terrible situations for our good, but mostly when he sent his Son to die for us. Look around. This world may be deteriorating rapidly, but there's still beauty for us to appreciate. When we see it, we know that a good God created it, not an evil force. It was evil that defiled this world and the goodness of God that redeemed humanity. When we experience pain, trauma, and darkness, it is easy to become jaded and hard-hearted. We may even struggle to see God's goodness, but it exists. All you have to do is take a little time to look for it.

Heavenly Father, thank you for being good to me. Forgive me for the many times I doubted your goodness. I see your goodness in my life daily, and I give you my life in return. Amen.

---

3 "The Water In You: Water And The Human Body," USGS Science for a Changing World, US Department of the Interior, accessed on August 5, 2020, https://www.usgs.gov.

This world is fallen and evil. How can you, as a child of God, mirror his goodness in this world?

Only goodness and faithful love will pursue me all the days of my life, and I will dwell in the house of the LORD as long as I live.

PSALM 23:6 HCSB

No doubt about it!
God is good—good to good people,
good to the good-hearted.

PSALM 73:1 MSG

Good comes to those who lend money generously and conduct their business fairly.

PSALM 112:5 NLT

This city will bear on My behalf a name of joy, praise, and glory before all the nations of the earth, who will hear of all the good I will do for them. They will tremble with awe because of all the good and all the peace I will bring about for them.

JEREMIAH 33:9 HCSB

GRACE

For human knowledge, defining grace is a difficult challenge. There are theological definitions, but I've yet to find an adequate description of God's beautiful gift of grace. To my mind, Justin Holcomb gives the best explanation: "Grace is the opposite of karma, which is all about getting what you deserve. Grace is getting what you don't deserve." We did not deserve redemption; we deserved death. That is the price of sin. But because of God's goodness and grace, we were redeemed through the price paid by Jesus. Think about John Newton, the author of the powerful hymn, "Amazing Grace." He was a slave trader and converted to Christianity during a voyage at sea. Newton immediately renounced slavery after his conversion and wrote the now well-known and beloved song billions learned when they came to Christ.[4] It is God's grace that rescues us in the darkest places of life, but his mercy is the reason we do not receive the consequences of those sins. Thank God for his amazing grace!

Heavenly Father, thank you for your amazing grace and for imparting into my life the many blessings I do not deserve. Your grace sustains me. Amen.

---

4   David Sheward, "The Real Story behind 'Amazing Grace,'" Biography, A&E Television Network, August 11, 2015, https://www.biography.com.

How do you define the grace of God, and can you see examples of his grace in your life?

Sunrise breaks through the darkness for good people—
God's grace and mercy and justice!

PSALM 112:4 MSG

Sin is no longer your master, for you no longer live under
the requirements of the law. Instead, you live under the
freedom of God's grace.

ROMANS 6:14 NLT

He said to me, "My grace is sufficient for you, for power
is perfected in weakness." Therefore, I will most gladly
boast all the more about my weaknesses, so that Christ's
power may reside in me.

2 CORINTHIANS 12:9 HCSB

This superabundant grace is already powerfully working
in us, releasing within us all forms of wisdom and
practical understanding.

EPHESIANS 1:8 TPT

The grace of God has appeared that offers salvation
to all people.

TITUS 2:11 NIV

GUIDANCE

Putting together a puzzle is not something I've ever been good at doing. Mainly because all the pieces are out of order, and it's hard to figure out where each fits perfectly. But such is life! We may not always see the pieces or even know where they are supposed to be placed, but God has strategically placed each one within reach. His Word is a perfect guidance for all areas of our lives. When we use Scripture as the lamp to our feet, guiding us through dark places, we begin to see these troubles from God's perspective. During challenging times, we may not see the full picture. And, in challenging times, we may not know how it's all going to work out. But, if we are faithful to obey his Word and lean on his wisdom and not our own understanding, we will live with the guidance of God's Holy Spirit, his living Word, and have peace through it all.

Heavenly Father, thank you for guiding my steps in all the days and nights of my service as a first responder. Lead me and let your Word be a lamp to the path I am on. Amen.

How can you use the Word of God as your guiding
light through this life?

You are my lamp, O LORD,
and my God lightens my darkness.

2 SAMUEL 22:29 ESV

That is what God is like.
He is our God forever and ever,
and he will guide us until we die.

PSALM 48:14 NLT

Whether you turn to the right or to the left,
your ears will hear a voice behind you, saying,
"This is the way; walk in it."

ISAIAH 30:21 NIV

He is the perfect Father who leads us all,
works through us all, and lives in us all!

EPHESIANS 4:6 TPT

HEALING

Over time, our physical bodies will begin to deteriorate. Many children have suffered due to various diseases, and it is never easy watching loved one's battle illness. When we think of healing, we often think of physical healing, but healing is much more than just our bodies being made whole. The most significant healing any person can experience is the healing of the soul, once diseased by sin, becoming cleansed by the blood of Jesus and made perfect for eternity. Sin is the greatest threat of disease to our souls, and the only antidote is the blood of Jesus. If we must live this life for a little while with physical sickness but live eternally with God, then the greatest healing was not for our physical bodies. God still heals our physical bodies, but we must not love him for healing he can give to these temporary vessels. We must love him for restoring our souls and for being the only way to eternal life.

Heavenly Father, thank you for healing my body of any illness, injury, or disease. I am grateful you are the healer. But most of all, thank you for healing my aching soul, riddled with the wounds of sin, redeemed by the blood of your Son, Jesus. Amen.

How can suffering in this life make you more like Christ, ultimately leading to your perfect, eternal healing?

When they are sick, God will restore them, lying upon their bed of suffering. He will raise them up again and restore them back to health.

PSALM 41:3 TPT

Heal me, LORD, and I will be healed;
save me and I will be saved,
for you are the one I praise.

JEREMIAH 17:14 NIV

A man with leprosy came and knelt in front of Jesus, begging to be healed. "If you are willing, you can heal me and make me clean," he said. Moved with compassion, Jesus reached out and touched him. "I am willing," he said. "Be healed!"

MARK 1:40–41 NLT

Are any of you sick? You should call for the elders of the church to come and pray over you, anointing you with oil in the name of the Lord. Such a prayer offered in faith will heal the sick, and the Lord will make you well. And if you have committed any sins, you will be forgiven.

JAMES 5:14–15 NLT

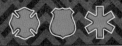

HEAVEN

When we think of heaven, it's common to wonder if we will see family and friends who have passed away before us or see faces from some of the most well-known names in the Bible, most notably, Jesus. I know what the Scriptures tell us heaven is like, but it's hard not to wonder. If you ask a dozen theologians to describe heaven, you'll likely get a few similar answers, but there will be some differences in doctrinal beliefs. Heaven is more than a state of mind or an earthly peace. Yes, I believe we (meaning the body of Christ) are supposed to live in such a way that promotes a little bit of heaven on earth, but there is an eternal reward destination. It's heaven. And while nobody has all the answers about this fantastic eternal reward, you can guarantee it'll be worth the wait.

Heavenly Father, thank you for being with me in this life and preparing a place for me in heaven. I look forward to spending time worshiping you for all eternity. Amen.

How can you live so your life connects others to an eternal reward in heaven?

Don't let your hearts be troubled. Trust in God, and trust also in me. There is more than enough room in my Father's home. If this were not so, would I have told you that I am going to prepare a place for you?

JOHN 14:1–2 NLT

We know that if the earthly tent we live in is destroyed, we have a building from God, an eternal house in heaven, not built by human hands.

2 CORINTHIANS 5:1 NIV

When the Messiah, who is your life, is revealed, then you also will be revealed with Him in glory.

COLOSSIANS 3:4 HCSB

They desire a better, that is, a heavenly country. Therefore God is not ashamed to be called their God, for He has prepared a city for them.

HEBREWS 11:16 NKJV

HELP

Throughout Scripture, we see numerous examples of God's help for his people. From the parting of the Red Sea to feeding the more than five thousand with a mere five loaves of bread and some fish, God proves his faithfulness time and time again. Think about the many times God has helped you. I bet if you start looking at examples of his help in your life, you will quickly lose count. If you are feeling lonely, he is your helper. If you are tired and weak, he is the source of strength. Again, he is your helper. When David was about to take on Goliath, he first sought the help of God. "So David inquired of the LORD, saying, 'Shall I go up against the Philistines? Will You deliver them into my hand?' And the LORD said to David, 'Go up, for I will doubtless deliver the Philistines into your hand'" (2 Samuel 5:19 NKJV). Before you encounter the battle, get to know your helper. Become familiar and well-acquainted with the one who will be with you.

Heavenly Father, thank you for always making a way, and when I am lacking physical strength, wisdom, or direction, you are my helper. When I am outnumbered, you help me. Amen.

Can you count the number of times God has been there to help you in challenging situations?

The LORD will fight for you,
and you have only to be silent.

EXODUS 14:14 ESV

You yourselves have seen everything the LORD your
God has done to all these nations for your sake;
it was the LORD your God who fought for you.

JOSHUA 23:3 NIV

Our help is in the name of the LORD,
the Maker of heaven and earth.

PSALM 124:8 NIV

I will strengthen you; I will help you;
I will hold on to you with My righteous right hand.

ISAIAH 41:10 HCSB

Let us come boldly to the throne of our gracious God.
There we will receive his mercy,
and we will find grace to help us when we need it most.

HEBREWS 4:16 NLT

HOLINESS

Holiness is still important to God. In the Old Testament alone, the word *holy* is mentioned more than four hundred times. Even in the New Testament, Scripture says in 1 Peter 1:16, "Be holy, because I am holy" (NIV). Too often, we try to achieve holiness through good behavior, but that is not enough. Nothing we can do in our might, on our best day, will get us remotely close to the slightest degree of holiness. It's only by the blood of Jesus, through his righteousness, that we are made holy. We've been set apart, called to be sanctified in Christ for his glory. Accept his gift, the gift of redemption and eternal life, and walk in the commandments he gave us. The only way to holiness is with Jesus in our hearts and his Word leading our lives.

Heavenly Father, I know I will never attain holiness in my own efforts. Wash me with the blood of your Son Jesus, and I will walk in the path of righteousness. Amen.

You have been set apart for his glory. How does
this affect the thoughts you entertain, the way you
speak, and future behaviors?

I am Yahweh, who brought you up from the land of Egypt
to be your God, so you must be holy because I am holy.

LEVITICUS 11:45 HCSB

Set yourselves apart to be holy, for I am the LORD your
God. Keep all my decrees by putting them into practice,
for I am the LORD who makes you holy.

LEVITICUS 20:7–8 NLT

You therefore must be perfect,
as your heavenly Father is perfect.

MATTHEW 5:48 ESV

God's will was for us to be made holy by the sacrifice
of the body of Jesus Christ, once for all time.

HEBREWS 10:10 NLT

HOLY SPIRIT

From the book of Genesis throughout the entirety of the Bible, we see the Holy Spirit's presence. The Holy Spirit is quite possibly the most misunderstood person of the Trinity but also the most personal. When Jesus ascended into heaven, he said he would send to us the Comforter, the Holy Spirit. And, in the book of Acts, we see the demonstration of the power of the Holy Spirit. Throughout Scripture, the Holy Spirit is the power behind men and women called to a divine purpose, a seemingly impossible mission. We don't have to ask God to let the Holy Spirit fall on us or even to come into our midst, for he dwells within every believer who asks him to. This is not some mystical force but the personal presence of the living God. Our job is to be kind hosts for the Holy Spirit and live in a way that does not grieve him but promotes his presence in our lives. Welcome the Holy Spirit into your life today.

Heavenly Father, thank you for giving me the Comforter, the Holy Spirit to empower me, comfort me, strengthen me, and guide me through life. Amen.

The Trinity is the Godhead three in one, the Father, Son, and Holy Spirit. How does the Holy Spirit help you through life?

Jesus replied, "I assure you, no one can enter the Kingdom of God without being born of water and the Spirit. Humans can reproduce only human life, but the Holy Spirit gives birth to spiritual life."

JOHN 3:5–6 NLT

The Father who knows all hearts knows what the Spirit is saying, for the Spirit pleads for us believers in harmony with God's own will.

ROMANS 8:27 NLT

Because you are his sons, God sent the Spirit of his Son into our hearts, the Spirit who calls out, "Abba, Father."

GALATIANS 4:6 NIV

All of us can come to the Father through the same Holy Spirit because of what Christ has done for us.

EPHESIANS 2:18 NLT

You have an anointing from the Holy One, and you know all things.

1 JOHN 2:20 NKJV

HOPE

We've all been guilty of placing our hope in the wrong source. We hope things will work out, or we hope others will do the right thing, but by doing this, we are setting ourselves up for disappointment. Most circumstances are outside our direct control, and we cannot govern what other people do. When we place our hope in God, we put our hope in an absolute. He is in control. We cannot have faith without hope, and hope cannot exist without faith. The source of these powerful elements of our relationship with God must be in him alone. When people who have no relationship with God speak of this hope, they are referring to a temporary version of it, one that is not promised or guaranteed. But as his children, our hope is founded, it is proven, and it is safe. Place your hope in Christ and walk in his grace today and always.

Heavenly Father, thank you for the eternal, perfect hope you have given me in this life. No matter the trials that come, no matter the challenges I will face, I know you have established a perfect hope for me. Amen.

In the middle of a world that is increasingly hostile toward Christians, how is the hope God has given you empowering as you walk in the path he has established before you?

You are the hope of everyone on earth,
even those who sail on distant seas.

PSALM 65:5 NLT

You are my refuge and my shield;
your word is my source of hope.

PSALM 119:114 NLT

I say: The LORD is my portion,
therefore I will put my hope in Him.

LAMENTATIONS 3:24 HCSB

Hope does not put us to shame, because God's love has been poured out into our hearts through the Holy Spirit, who has been given to us.

ROMANS 5:5 NIV

We who have run for our very lives to God have every reason to grab the promised hope with both hands and never let go. It's an unbreakable spiritual lifeline.

HEBREWS 6:18–19 MSG

IDENTITY

Often society pressures us to define ourselves based on our profession or social status. But when we fail, these role-based identities are fractured. Defining one's identity based on external measures is temporary and extremely fragile. We must establish our identity from our internal beliefs and our relationship with God, not our role in this world. This approach requires us to abandon some negative belief patterns that limit us to the ceiling this world will place us under. The world may try to define you based on limited and temporary situations. One encounter with God will change your identity from a sinner to redeemed. Just like God changed Jacob's name to Israel, he will be the source of your true identity. If he can change Saul to Paul on the road to Damascus, he can change the identity of any of us from a roughneck sinner to a man or woman after his own heart.

Heavenly Father, never let me forget my identity is in you and the perfect sacrifice of your Son. In my moments of confusion, remind me you call me your own. Amen.

What direction and clarity does having your identity
in Christ provide?

You created my inmost being;
you knit me together in my mother's womb.

PSALM 139:13 NIV

God who made you has something to say to you;
the God who formed you in the womb wants to help you.

ISAIAH 44:2 MSG

It is through him that we live and function and have our
identity; just as your own poets have said, "Our lineage
comes from him."

ACTS 17:28 TPT

Could it be any clearer that our former identity is now
and forever deprived of its power? For we were co-
crucified with him to dismantle the stronghold of sin
within us, so that we would not continue to live one
moment longer submitted to sin's power.

ROMANS 6:6 TPT

We are God's masterpiece. He has created us anew in
Christ Jesus, so we can do the good things he planned
for us long ago.

EPHESIANS 2:10 NLT

IDOLATRY

Idols aren't always readily visible before our eyes. They aren't limited to statues we've carved out or built to worship. The fact is, anything and anyone in our lives can become an idol. Idolatry is the practice of elevating something or someone above God. While it is often defined as the worship of a physical object, it can also simply mean an extreme devotion to someone other than God. Do you love your family more than you love God? What about your career? Often, when we are stressed, we give more time to the concern than we do to God. Don't allow the world's worries to become your god, an idol that consumes your time, takes your attention, and receives your worship. Anything is liable to become an idol in our lives if we're not careful to check our hearts and motives or the amount of time and attention we give them. Tear down the idols in your life and put the one true God back on the throne of your heart.

Heavenly Father, tear down every idol I have established in my heart, either knowingly or unknowingly. You are my Lord, the only King of my heart. Amen.

Can you identify any potential idols in your life?
How can you remove them?

You must not make for yourself an idol of any kind, or
an image of anything in the heavens or on the earth or
in the sea. You must not bow down to them or worship
them, for I, the LORD your God, am a jealous God who
will not tolerate your affection for any other gods. I lay
the sins of the parents upon their children; the entire
family is affected—even children in the third and fourth
generations of those who reject me.

DEUTERONOMY 5:8–9 NLT

Because they have forsaken me and burned incense to
other gods and aroused my anger by all the idols their
hands have made, my anger will burn against this place
and will not be quenched.

2 KINGS 22:17 NIV

Those who trust in idols, who say to images,
"You are our gods," will be turned back in utter shame.

ISAIAH 42:17 NIV

JESUS

In a world where so many want to give you a five-step plan to success, Jesus is not preached front and center as often as he should be. The only reason we have hope is because God so loved the world that he sent his only Son, Jesus (see John 3:16.) Jesus is the one hope for humanity. He came, born of a virgin, died on a cross, and rose on the third day. He is the only way to a reconciled relationship with the heavenly Father and the only way to eternal life. When we read the Bible, we must not read it as a story with ourselves as the primary character but rather as a love letter from heaven, where the greatest ransom for sin was ever paid by one who came as man but remained fully God, all for you and me. That's Jesus. He's not a mythical figure or merely a great historical figure, but he is a living Savior who loved us enough to leave his throne in heaven to give his life for us. He's my best friend, and he can be yours too.

Heavenly Father, thank you for sending your only Son, Jesus, to die for me. Because of him, I have been set free. I want to live in a way that honors Jesus and is pleasing to you. Amen.

What role does Jesus have in your life as a first responder and all other roles you have in life?

I am the good shepherd. I know My own sheep, and they know Me, as the Father knows Me, and I know the Father. I lay down My life for the sheep.

JOHN 10:14–15 HCSB

Jesus explained, "I am the Way, I am the Truth, and I am the Life. No one comes next to the Father except through union with me. To know me is to know my Father too."

JOHN 14:6 TPT

Everyone in Israel can know for certain that Jesus, whom you crucified, is the one God has made both Lord and the Messiah.

ACTS 2:36 TPT

There is one God, and there is one mediator between God and men, the man Christ Jesus, who gave himself as a ransom for all, which is the testimony given at the proper time.

1 TIMOTHY 2:5–6 ESV

JUSTICE

When you hear the word *justice*, you may think of the Department of Justice, criminal justice, or the Pledge of Allegiance to the flag: "One Nation under God, indivisible, with liberty and justice for all." We can turn on the news or read news publications, and it won't take long to see the number of injustices in the world. How do we prioritize them? We begin with the ones we can control and by knowing God hates injustice in our society. Deuteronomy 27:19 says, "Cursed is the one who perverts the justice due the stranger, the fatherless, and widow" (NKJV). If addressing injustice is within our power and authority, we will be held accountable for how we deal with these issues. As Americans, we know this is the land of "justice for all," but as Christians, we know the higher authority is God, his Word, and the standards he has established. Don't turn a blind eye to injustice for the sake of avoiding conflict.

Heavenly Father, thank you for the courage and wisdom to address injustice. May my heart always be sensitive to your convictions and my decisions as a first responder be honorable to your name. Amen.

The number of injustices in this world are many, but men and women who are willing to be heaven's hands and feet on this earth can bring hope to others. How can you, as a first responder, address these issues?

Let the fear of the LORD be on you. Judge carefully, for with the LORD our God there is no injustice or partiality or bribery.

2 CHRONICLES 19:7 NIV

He does not let the wicked live but gives justice to the afflicted.

JOB 36:6 NLT

You're a God who makes things right, giving justice to the defenseless.

PSALM 103:6 TPT

Justice will rule in the wilderness and righteousness in the fertile field.

ISAIAH 32:16 NLT

Do not take revenge, my dear friends, but leave room for God's wrath, for it is written: "It is mine to avenge; I will repay," says the Lord.

ROMANS 12:19 NIV

LEADERSHIP

The coauthor of this book, Adam Davis, and his brother, Brandon, were having a conversation about leadership and manhood. Brandon made a profound statement on the matter. He said, "So often, people spend their lives trying to fix all these problems this machine is spitting out. It is car trouble, career trouble, relationship trouble, and all their time and energy is spent trying to fix these problems. The real effort should be in fixing the machine spitting out all the problems." We cannot lead our families, teams, or others if we are not willing first to follow the lead of Jesus and let him fix "this machine." You won't have to search long to find several books on leadership, but the best lesson you can study on the topic is the life of Jesus. Humility, serving, and selflessness are the core principles, but they must all be powered by the proper love. Leadership isn't about titles or positions. It's about being the best servant with the purest heart and the cleanest motives and letting Jesus fix the machine that spits out the problems.

Heavenly Father, thank you for giving me the best example of leadership. I know I cannot lead others until I lead myself and submit to you. Amen.

Leadership is one of the most talked about topics in business and sales. It is too often lacking in the family environment and personal development. How can leadership beginning in your own life help you be a better leader elsewhere?

Commission Joshua, and encourage and strengthen him, for he will lead this people across and will cause them to inherit the land that you will see.

DEUTERONOMY 3:28 NIV

God commanded Joshua son of Nun saying,
"Be strong. Take courage.
You will lead the People of Israel
into the land I promised to give them.
And I'll be right there with you."

DEUTERONOMY 31:23 MSG

The LORD told Joshua, "Today I will begin to make you a great leader in the eyes of all the Israelites. They will know that I am with you, just as I was with Moses."

JOSHUA 3:7 NLT

I will raise up for myself a faithful priest, who will do according to what is in my heart and mind. I will firmly establish his priestly house, and they will minister before my anointed one always.

1 SAMUEL 2:35 NIV

LIFE

Every life has a beginning and an end, no matter the length of time in between. If you are given the opportunity to live a long, healthy life and serve as a first responder, live it well. Use it fully. Don't spend your days complaining and being miserable. This life *will* end, but what matters is what you do for eternity. The greatest gift we've been given is when God the Father sent his only Son, Jesus, to die for us. He did this so we could have eternal life if only we would accept this gift. This life is a gift. And one day it will end. What will you do with yours? It is ok to set up wealth for your family and pursue great success in your career, but what matters most is the effect you have on the lives of others for eternity. Eternity is a long time. Don't leave this life with regret.

Heavenly Father, thank you for giving me life and life to the fullest through your Son. Give me wisdom to make the best decisions, discernment to know which way to go, and ears to hear your still, small voice. Amen.

The greatest thing you can do is invest in the lives of others for eternity. How can you use your life to invest in others for eternal life?

The LORD gives both death and life;
he brings some down to the grave but raises others up.
1 SAMUEL 2:6 NLT

If you walk in obedience to me and keep my decrees
and commands as David your father did,
I will give you a long life.
1 KINGS 3:14 NIV

With You is the fountain of life;
In Your light we see light.
PSALM 36:9 NKJV

Eat your food with joy, and drink your wine
with a happy heart, for God approves of this!
ECCLESIASTES 9:7 NLT

Your old life is dead.
Your new life, which is your real life—
even though invisible to spectators—
is with Christ in God. He is your life.
COLOSSIANS 3:3 MSG

LONELINESS

These days, we often gauge our social status by how many followers or "friends" we have on social media, and that has led to an illusion of social connectedness and healthy relationships. However, the opposite is true. Studies have shown that Americans are lonelier now than ever before. Loneliness can lead to a number of issues, including a decrease in cognitive function and eventually depression.[5] We may be required to adapt to solitude at some point in life, but the reality is that we are never alone as followers of Jesus. He has promised throughout his Word that he will never leave or forsake us. Being part of the body of Christ means we have earthly relationships, and knowing how to establish boundaries, have healthy relationships, and navigate those relationships will help us maintain healthy social connectedness. You are never alone with Jesus as the captain of your life.

Heavenly Father, I know that with you in my life, I am never alone. No longer do I have to feel alone when I am by myself or with others. My focus is on you, and I can be a better first responder because of this fact. Amen.

---

5   "Signs and Symptoms of Chronic Loneliness," Cigna, March 2019, https://www.cigna.com.

When you know you are never alone because of the
God you serve, how does it position you to be a
better servant, spouse, parent, friend, and person?

Be strong and courageous.
Do not fear or be in dread of them,
for it is the LORD your God who goes with you.
He will not leave you or forsake you.

DEUTERONOMY 31:6 ESV

The LORD himself goes before you and will be with you;
he will never leave you nor forsake you.
Do not be afraid; do not be discouraged.

DEUTERONOMY 31:8 NIV

Father to the fatherless, defender of widows—this is God,
whose dwelling is holy. God places the lonely in families;
he sets the prisoners free and gives them joy. But he
makes the rebellious live in a sun-scorched land.

PSALM 68:5–6 NLT

LOVE

The cure for all that ails humanity is the love of God. When we love others as he has loved us, and when we live a life that demonstrates the love of God in all we do, we open the door for others to experience Jesus for themselves. It is love that changes the hard, cold hearts of humanity. It is love that motivates selfless men and women to lay their lives down for their friends and even for complete strangers. There's no greater love than the love Jesus showed us by giving his life on the cross to pay for our sins. No other action by any other human being will come remotely close to what Jesus did for us. But we can live in a way that makes others want to know about this love. We will never lead a lost world to a living God without demonstrating his love in a real way.

Heavenly Father, your love has changed me. It has redeemed me. It has set me free. May my life be a demonstration of your love in all I do, and may I lead others to know your Son, Jesus. Amen.

How can you demonstrate the love of Jesus
to others today?

Your unfailing love is better than life itself;
how I praise you!

Psalm 63:3 nlt

A new command I give you: Love one another.
As I have loved you, so you must love one another.
By this everyone will know that you are my disciples,
if you love one another.

John 13:34–35 niv

Three things will last forever—
faith, hope, and love—
and the greatest of these is love.

1 Corinthians 13:13 nlt

Above all, maintain an intense love for each other,
since love covers a multitude of sins.

1 Peter 4:8 hcsb

If we love one another, God dwells deeply within us,
and his love becomes complete in us—perfect love!

1 John 4:12 msg

MERCY

If somehow in the world of imagination, we met before being born in this life, I would see our conversation going something like this. "Listen, there are some tools we need to make it out and get back here. Pack the grace of God. We're going to mess up. We're going to sin, and that will hurt God, but he's given us a pretty good dose of forgiveness for the journey. But there are two more things we need to be sure to take with us: his mercy and favor. His mercy is magnificent. It is brand new every morning, unchanging. But his favor will get us places we could never get on our own." Mercy is when we do not receive the punishment we deserve. Grace empowers us to get through something we cannot do on our own and receive what we did not earn. His mercy is new every morning. It never ages, and it never runs dry. Accept this beautiful gift from God today!

Heavenly Father, thank you for new mercy every morning. For an unending supply. May I never take for granted your mercy. Amen.

How can you live in a way that demonstrates
gratitude for God's mercy in your life?

As the heavens are high above the earth,
So great is His mercy toward those who fear Him.

PSALM 103:11 NKJV

His mercy extends to those who fear him,
from generation to generation.

LUKE 1:50 NIV

Because of his great love for us, God, who is rich in
mercy, made us alive with Christ even when we were dead
in transgressions—it is by grace you have been saved.

EPHESIANS 2:4–5 NIV

I will be merciful to their unrighteousness, and their
sins and their lawless deeds I will remember no more.

HEBREWS 8:12 NKJV

There will be no mercy for those who have not shown
mercy to others. But if you have been merciful, God will
be merciful when he judges you.

JAMES 2:13 NLT

OBEDIENCE

When we obey the Word of God, we position ourselves to walk in his blessing and favor. But there are times we must discern the still, small voice of the Holy Spirit directing us to do things in this life that may not be defined explicitly in his Word. It's a given to obey God's Word, the Great Commandment to love him and love others, but it is not always so cut and dried. At times, it means buying a meal for someone, telling someone the good news of God's love, or directly calling a friend or loved one who may be going through something difficult in life. God honors our obedience, but delayed obedience is the same as disobedience, and he desires our willful obedience to his leading more than our sacrifices. What is he calling you to do?

Heavenly Father, through all my life, may I remain obedience-focused and not outcome-focused. I know when I am obedient to your Word, I walk in safety and freedom. Amen.

Why do you think obedience is more desirable to God than sacrifice?

Obey my laws and live by my decrees.
I am your God. Keep my decrees and laws:
The person who obeys them lives by them. I am God.
LEVITICUS 18:5 MSG

I lavish unfailing love for a thousand generations on
those who love me and obey my commands.
DEUTERONOMY 5:10 NLT

Blessed rather are those who hear
the word of God and obey it.
LUKE 11:28 NIV

You show that you are my intimate friends
when you obey all that I command you.
JOHN 15:14 TPT

Anyone who does not remain in Christ's teaching but
goes beyond it, does not have God. The one who remains
in that teaching, this one has both the Father and the Son.
2 JOHN 9 HCSB

PATIENCE

Going on road trips with children is often an adventure and a real test of patience, not only for the adults but also for the children. Children often ask repeatedly, "Are we there yet?" To them, the trip may seem like it is longer than it is, but as adults, we know where we are going, we know the next turns and how many more miles until we reach the destination. You see, we have all the details, in most cases, the entire itinerary. Patience is required in trying times when we need an answer or solution but lack all the information about our circumstances. Having faith in God means we trust his timing, and we also trust him with all the details we may not be privy to at the moment. We develop patience as we mature, but God is not bothered by our repeatedly asking, "Are we there yet?" He encourages us to approach him with childlike faith instead of talking to him with our intellect.

Heavenly Father, thank you for being patient with me, and I know patience is a virtue of love. May my life resemble the longsuffering and patience you have shown me. Amen.

In what areas of your life can you practice patience more consistently?

Guide me in Your truth and teach me,
for You are the God of my salvation;
I wait for You all day long.

PSALM 25:5 HCSB

For you, O LORD, do I wait;
it is you, O LORD my God, who will answer.

PSALM 38:15 ESV

I will look to the LORD;
I will wait for the God of my salvation;
My God will hear me.

MICAH 7:7 NKJV

The Lord does not delay His promise, as some
understand delay, but is patient with you, not wanting
any to perish but all to come to repentance.

2 PETER 3:9 HCSB

Remember, our Lord's patience
gives people time to be saved.

2 PETER 3:15 NLT

PEACE

A question has been debated over the ages, often without an adequate answer: What is the cost of peace? According to a 2012 report from the Institute for Economics and Peace, the price is $9.46 trillion.[6] Or rather, that is the cost that governments of the world have paid to contain violence. However, what these nations and governments seek is not the same peace we seek internally as human beings. Yes, it is a fact that we can have peace in our hearts, minds, and souls, while the world around us crumbles before our eyes. The overwhelming, unspeakable peace of God is available for us whether we are enduring terrible hardships or traumatic situations. The source of global peace may well rest in governmental leaders, military service members, and voters. But the true, unmatched peace of humanity has its source in a relationship with Jesus, and the Holy Spirit is our comforter. This peace means the difference between having a mind in turmoil and navigating the storms of this world with ease. Discover the peace of God, walk in it, and enjoy a new standard of living.

Heavenly Father, your peace is the perfect antidote to the storms of this life. Fill my heart and mind with your peace now and forever. Amen.

6   "The Economic Cost of Violence Containment: a Comprehensive Assessment of the Global Cost of Violence," Institute for Economics and Peace, May 2015, https://www.economicsandpeace.org.

How does the peace of God keep you through the storms of life?

The effect of righteousness will be peace, and the result of righteousness, quietness and trust forever.

ISAIAH 32:17 ESV

God blesses those who work for peace, for they will be called the children of God.

MATTHEW 5:9 NLT

Peace I leave with you; my peace I give you. I do not give to you as the world gives. Do not let your hearts be troubled and do not be afraid.

JOHN 14:27 NIV

Since we have been made right in God's sight by faith, we have peace with God because of what Jesus Christ our Lord has done for us.

ROMANS 5:1 NLT

Do not be anxious about anything, but in every situation, by prayer and petition, with thanksgiving, present your requests to God. And the peace of God, which transcends all understanding, will guard your hearts and your minds in Christ Jesus.

PHILIPPIANS 4:6–7 NIV

PERSECUTION

Americans from various walks of life have experienced persecution throughout our history. It isn't always violent acts toward individuals or groups based on their beliefs or views in life. Sometimes it's passive hostility. It could be ill-treatment, verbal abuse, or physical violence, solely because of your skin color, religious beliefs, political views, or other deeply held convictions. Law enforcement officers face persecution for their chosen professions, as do other first responders. Christians will face increased persecution in years to come as such persecution has grown exponentially over the past decade. How we respond to this issue can define the course of our lives. Persecution requires the heart of a warrior who relentlessly pursues completing the mission assigned. It requires every Christian to be enduring, persevering, all while serving with a heart motivated by perfect love. Persecution will come, and when it does, will you continue standing and persevere?

Heavenly Father, there will be a time when my faith is tested, when my heart is tried, and I want to be prepared for that moment. Help me, when that day is at hand, to stand, to be faithful to you. Amen.

How can faith in God help you to remain steadfast
in the face of persecution?

Blessed are those who are persecuted because of
righteousness, for theirs is the kingdom of heaven.

MATTHEW 5:10 NIV

When people accuse you before everyone and forcefully
drag you before the religious leaders and authorities, do
not be troubled. Don't worry about defending yourself
or be concerned about how to answer their accusations.
Simply be confident and allow the Spirit of Wisdom
access to your heart, and he will reveal in that very
moment what you are to say to them.

LUKE 12:11—12 TPT

God will use this persecution to show his justice and
to make you worthy of his Kingdom, for which you are
suffering. In his justice he will pay back those who
persecute you.

2 THESSALONIANS 1:5—6 NLT

All who desire to live a godly life in Christ Jesus will be
persecuted, while evil people and impostors will go on
from bad to worse, deceiving and being deceived.

2 TIMOTHY 3:12—13 ESV

PERSEVERANCE

One of the most challenging things you will do in this life is commit to following Christ. This world is a fallen place, full of evil, and if you remain on the sidelines of life and live your own way, you will likely have less trouble. You're no threat to the enemy that way. But there's a need for followers of Christ to persevere and endure challenges, not to cower in times of hardship and stress. You may not receive healing immediately after praying for it. You may not receive that job or financial relief the first time you ask God to help you. And you may not see many other answers to your prayers immediately. God's not a slot machine. Faith requires action rooted in obedience. The key is to persevere through the difficulties even when you do not achieve immediate success. Keep walking the path God has put you on, remain faithful with the gifts and responsibilities you've been given, and in due season, you will reap a reward.

Heavenly Father, in the times of great challenges, give me the strength and willpower to endure and persevere so my life may honor your name and bring glory to you. Amen.

What steps can you take to endure through trying times?

We have become companions of the Messiah if we hold firmly until the end the reality that we had at the start.

HEBREWS 3:14 HCSB

You have need of endurance,
so that after you have done the will of God,
you may receive the promise.

HEBREWS 10:36 NKJV

The one who looks intently into the perfect law of freedom and perseveres in it, and is not a forgetful hearer but one who does good works—this person will be blessed in what he does.

JAMES 1:25 HCSB

Because you have obeyed my command to persevere, I will protect you from the great time of testing that will come upon the whole world to test those who belong to this world.

REVELATION 3:10 NLT

POWER

The words *power* and *strength* are often used interchangeably, but there is a difference. Simply put, power is the ability to do something, and strength is the force or might behind that ability. Similarly, you can have power and still lack authority. To walk in God's power means to walk in his ability and to rely on his strength through prayer, worship, and Bible study. God created humanity for community and companionship, not isolation. Even with great friends and family, we should remember our source of power is not rooted in flesh and blood but in God's spirit. When we intentionally and consistently recharge our hearts and minds through prayer and time spent studying the Bible, we remain connected to the power source. If you feel like you cannot complete the mission he has called you to do, remember that before God called you to do it, he equipped you with the power (ability) and strength (might) to accomplish those things.

Heavenly Father, I rely on the power of the Holy Spirit to propel me through this life, through all the peaks and valleys. Strengthen me, empower me, fill me with your spirit with every breath I take. Amen.

Without God's power in our lives, we cannot overcome sin. How does his power elevate you to victorious living?

It is not for you to know the times or dates the Father has set by his own authority. But you will receive power when the Holy Spirit comes on you; and you will be my witnesses in Jerusalem, and in all Judea and Samaria, and to the ends of the earth.

ACTS 1:7–8 NIV

He was crucified in weakness, but He lives by God's power. For we also are weak in Him, yet toward you we will live with Him by God's power.

2 CORINTHIANS 13:4 HCSB

God will never give you the spirit of fear, but the Holy Spirit who gives you mighty power, love, and self-control.

2 TIMOTHY 1:7 TPT

His divine power has given us everything we need for a godly life through our knowledge of him who called us by his own glory and goodness.

2 PETER 1:3 NIV

PRAYER

One of the most common questions new and even sea-
soned Christians ask is "How do I pray?" We tend to
overcomplicate this issue. I suppose there's something
about talking to the Creator of the universe that seems
intimidating. But he doesn't see it that way. In fact, Jesus
taught us how to pray in Matthew 6. He began his prayer
by acknowledging God as heavenly Father, and then he
blessed his name. When we begin all of our prayers with
a need or asking for something from God, it doesn't make
for a good relationship. Think about how you would feel if
your kids only talked to you when they needed something.
That's not the way to build a relationship or maintain one.
Prayer should be about listening to God as much as we
talk to him. It should also be a time that we verbally (in
faith) forgive those who have offended us and ask for forgiveness for our sins. This is a beautiful time to surrender
issues, and ourselves, to God daily. He's always listening.

*Heavenly Father, thank you for the open line of
communication to praise you, to confide in you, to intercede
for others, and to fellowship with you in worship. Amen.*

How can a healthy prayer life improve your mindset, thoughts, words, and actions?

What other nation is so great as to have their gods near them the way the LORD our God is near us whenever we pray to him?

DEUTERONOMY 4:7 NIV

You will call on me and come and pray to me, and I will listen to you. You will seek me and find me when you seek me with all your heart.

JEREMIAH 29:12–13 NIV

So it is with your prayers. Ask and you'll receive. Seek and you'll discover. Knock on heaven's door, and it will one day open for you. Every persistent person will get what he asks for. Every persistent seeker will discover what he needs. And everyone who knocks persistently will one day find an open door.

LUKE 11:9–10 TPT

Confess and acknowledge how you have offended one another and then pray for one another to be instantly healed, for tremendous power is released through the passionate, heartfelt prayer of a godly believer!

JAMES 5:16 TPT

PROTECTION

John 16:33 offers us profound assurance of God's protection in this life. Jesus said, "In this world you will have trouble. But take heart! I have overcome the world" (NIV). Yes, he has provided us with everything we need to be victorious in this world, but God's concern is more with our souls than our bodies. When we think about protection, it is often associated with the threats in this life. However, the most significant risks are not to our physical bodies, earthly lives, or material possessions but to the things we cannot touch or see. When we abide in God's presence and walk in his Word, we receive a hedge of protection for our peace and joy. God often protects things we don't see readily from threats we aren't aware of. The gift of discernment is invaluable, so follow the still, small voice of God. When you do, you will walk in the protection of God.

Heavenly Father, thank you for your Word, for wisdom, and for your protection over all aspects of my life. Open my eyes to the strategies of the enemy and protect me from his attacks. Amen.

How can walking with Jesus protect you from the attacks of the enemy?

No one will be able to stand against you all the days
of your life. As I was with Moses, so I will be with you;
I will never leave you nor forsake you.

JOSHUA 1:5 NIV

Pull me from the trap my enemies set for me,
for I find protection in you alone.

PSALM 31:4 NLT

He only is my rock and my salvation;
He is my defense; I shall not be moved.

PSALM 62:6 NKJV

Every word of God proves true.
He is a shield to all who come to him for protection.

PROVERBS 30:5 NLT

Everyone then who hears these words of mine and does
them will be like a wise man who built his house on the
rock. And the rain fell, and the floods came, and the
winds blew and beat on that house, but it did not fall,
because it had been founded on the rock.

MATTHEW 7:24–25 ESV

PURPOSE

Too often, we get so caught up in our earthly purpose that we forget God created us for an eternal purpose. The primary purpose of our existence is to live in such a way that exemplifies the kingdom of God here in our world, in this generation, reaching others with the love of God. After he gathered the twelve disciples, Jesus instructed them on how to replicate his ministry by saying, "Heal the sick, raise the dead, cleanse those who have leprosy, drive out demons. Freely you have received; freely give" (Matthew 10:8 NIV). We've lost our way as the "church" and have gotten caught up in doctrinal disagreements and vocational complications. Paul warns us, "Whatever you do, do it from the heart" (Colossians 3:23 CSB). But your purpose isn't tied up in an occupation. It's in God's presence where you discover your purpose, and from there, a career is just another vehicle for fulfilling what God created you to do. Never let the world cause you to be confused about the purpose for which God created you.

Heavenly Father, if I lose my way in this world and forget what you called me to do in this life, remind me the eternal kingdom-minded purpose for which you created me. Amen.

How can you align your kingdom purpose with
a vocation in the marketplace?

He is the one who will build a house for my Name. He will
be my son, and I will be his father. And I will establish
the throne of his kingdom over Israel forever.

1 CHRONICLES 22:10 NIV

His destiny-plan for the earth stands sure.
His forever-plan remains in place and will never fail.

PSALM 33:11 TPT

The LORD works everything together to accomplish his
purpose. Even the wicked are included in his plans—
he sets them aside for the day of disaster.

PROVERBS 16:4 TPT

The earth and sky will wear out and fade away
before one word I speak loses its power
or fails to accomplish its purpose.

MATTHEW 24:35 TPT

We are convinced that every detail of our lives is
continually woven together to fit into God's perfect plan
of bringing good into our lives, for we are his lovers who
have been called to fulfill his designed purpose.

ROMANS 8:28 TPT

RECONCILIATION

The Bible is clear: "All have sinned and fall short of the glory of God" (Romans 3:23 CSB). Not all offense is the same, but forgiveness is available to all who will accept and receive it. It is not our position to withhold forgiveness from others, as we are beneficiaries of God's mercy. When he looks at us, he sees us through his Son, and that is how we should see our brothers and sisters in Christ. Forgiveness and reconciliation are not the same, but we cannot experience reconciliation without first forgiving. The sin of Adam and Eve in the Garden of Eden destroyed the relationship between humanity and God, so God sent his Son to reconcile that relationship. While all relationships on earth will not be reconciled due to sin, forgiveness is still required, and it is an element of salvation. Reconciliation is available between you and God. It's been paid for and is ready for you to accept today.

Heavenly Father, thank you for restoring the relationship between you and me. I ask for forgiveness for any unaddressed sin in my life, both known and unknown. I forgive others who have offended me and release those offenses to you. Amen.

Not all relationships will be reconciled on earth, but how can you experience peace with God through forgiveness and reconciliation with him?

We also rejoice in God through our Lord Jesus Christ, through whom we have now received reconciliation.

ROMANS 5:11 ESV

Everything is from God, who reconciled us to Himself through Christ and gave us the ministry of reconciliation.

2 CORINTHIANS 5:18 HCSB

Once you were alienated from God and were enemies in your minds because of your evil behavior. But now he has reconciled you by Christ's physical body through death to present you holy in his sight, without blemish and free from accusation.

COLOSSIANS 1:21–22 NIV

REDEMPTION

It is not because of our works or goodness that redemption is possible. Rather, it is because of the love of God, his loving-kindness for us. When we deserved the worst punishment for our sins, he stepped in and paid the price to redeem us once and for all. Our old lives, our pasts, are now testimonies of his faithfulness and mercy demonstrated toward us. We were once slaves to sin and death, but Jesus ransomed us; he set us free from the bondage and gave us new life. Through the atonement of the bloodshed of Jesus, we now have a mission as a part of the church. Our commission from heaven is to live in a way that reflects his love, to show others how he changed us by the way we live our lives, and to lead others to experience his love and accept the payment Jesus made for all.

Heavenly Father, it is because of your love for me that I am redeemed. Grant me strength, courage, and willpower to live a life that honors and reflects the love you've shown me. Amen.

Having experienced the redemption of God, how can you live in a way that honors him and leads others to him?

It was not because you were more in number than any other people that the LORD set his love on you and chose you, for you were the fewest of all peoples, but it is because the LORD loves you and is keeping the oath that he swore to your fathers, that the LORD has brought you out with a mighty hand and redeemed you from the house of slavery, from the hand of Pharaoh king of Egypt.

DEUTERONOMY 7:7–8 ESV

He gave Himself for us to redeem us from all lawlessness and to cleanse for Himself a people for His own possession, eager to do good works.

TITUS 2:14 HCSB

Christ has now become the High Priest over all the good things that have come. He has entered that greater, more perfect Tabernacle in heaven, which was not made by human hands and is not part of this created world. With his own blood—not the blood of goats and calves— he entered the Most Holy Place once for all time and secured our redemption forever.

HEBREWS 9:11–12 NLT

REPENTANCE

The word *repentance* may cause you to wince, having heard it misused in various sermons in the past. But repentance leads to healing and reconciliation with Christ. Repentance results in a changed heart, a changed mind, a one-hundred-eighty degree turn from the direction you were heading in life. It's not doom and gloom. Instead, it's the first step to a beautiful walk with Jesus that leads to freedom and overwhelming victory in life. Repentance is not without its struggles, as the enemy (Satan) would love nothing more than to discourage and destroy you. He'll cause you to think things like, *Who do you think you are? After all the sinful things you've done, God doesn't want you!* The enemy is a great deceiver and a liar—the father of lies. A call to repentance isn't the hellfire and brimstone message of some sermons. It transitions you to a life of freedom and eternal life with God.

Heavenly Father, by the power of your Holy Spirit, help me to remain sensitive to your heart, and when I need repentance in my own life, help me to be quick to repent and change my heart. Amen.

How can repentance help you maintain a heart after
God and keep your conscience clean and clear?

The LORD is close to all whose hearts are crushed by pain,
and he is always ready to restore the repentant one.

PSALM 34:18 TPT

In repentance and rest is your salvation,
in quietness and trust is your strength.

ISAIAH 30:15 NIV

I take no pleasure in the death of anyone,
declares the Sovereign LORD. Repent and live!

EZEKIEL 18:32 NIV

Godly sorrow produces repentance leading to salvation,
not to be regretted; but the sorrow of the world
produces death.

2 CORINTHIANS 7:10 NKJV

Remember, therefore, what you have received and heard;
hold it fast, and repent. But if you do not wake up, I will
come like a thief, and you will not know at what time I
will come to you.

REVELATION 3:3 NIV

REST

It's estimated that between fifty and seventy million Americans regularly struggle with getting adequate sleep at night. Lack of sleep and rest leads us to experience further health related issues.[7] But rest is not a suggestion in the Bible. It is a requirement. Some refer to it as the Sabbath rest. First responders are not afforded time off every Sunday, the day most people associate with the Sabbath. The key here is finding time during the week to rest but also discovering the secret to the perfect peace of God that gives us great rest in our lives. We need physical rest, rest from service, from labor, from trials, but we also need to access the peace of God that gives us strength through times when physical rest is not possible due to long hours. Rest is found in Jesus, abiding by his words, obeying his commands, and walking with him. This means we give him our burdens in exchange for supernatural rest because of our faith and trust in him.

Heavenly Father, thank you for offering me rest in exchange for me giving you my burdens and cares. I accept the offer! I willingly give you my burdens and ask for your strength and peace to sustain me. Lead me to a place of rest in you.

---

7   "Sleep and Sleep Disorder Statistics," American Sleep Association, accessed on September 14, 2020, https://www.sleepassociation.org.

How can you be more diligent in getting
proper physical rest and also learn to rest
in the peace of God?

Remember what Moses the LORD's servant commanded
you when he said, "The LORD your God will give you rest,
and He will give you this land."

JOSHUA 1:13 HCSB

Blessed be the Lord, who has given rest to His people
Israel, according to all that He promised. There has
not failed one word of all His good promise, which He
promised through His servant Moses.

1 KINGS 8:56 NKJV

Those who live in the shelter of the Most High
will find rest in the shadow of the Almighty.

PSALM 91:1 NLT

SACRIFICE

In the Old Testament, God's people were required to present burnt offerings as a sacrifice for their sins. This requirement was null and void when the perfect sacrifice, the Lamb of God, Jesus, died on the cross for the sins of all humanity. We are not required to die for the sins of others to be washed clean, but there are other sacrifices in this world that are required of us. We can be grateful for the blood of Christ blotting out the sin of all who will accept and receive his sacrifice. You may be required to sacrifice time with your family to serve your nation or community, or you may be required to sacrifice doing something you want for a higher and better purpose in life. The perfect sacrifice is Jesus, and while he does not require us to physically give our lives to pay for our sins, he does demand us as a daily, living sacrifice, to die to our own desires and will in exchange for his.

Heavenly Father, thank you for the perfect sacrifice of your Son, Jesus. Thank you for empowering me to overcome my own will and fleshly desires to pursue your perfect will in my life. Amen.

What are some sacrifices you have made for others and God?

There is still much more to say of his unfailing love for us! For through the blood of Jesus we have heard the powerful declaration, "You are now righteous in my sight." And because of the sacrifice of Jesus, you will never experience the wrath of God.

ROMANS 5:9 TPT

God made Christ, who never sinned, to be the offering for our sin, so that we could be made right with God through Christ.

2 CORINTHIANS 5:21 NLT

Unlike those other high priests, he does not need to offer sacrifices every day. They did this for their own sins first and then for the sins of the people. But Jesus did this once for all when he offered himself as the sacrifice for the people's sins.

HEBREWS 7:27 NLT

By his one perfect sacrifice he made us perfectly holy and complete for all time!

HEBREWS 10:14 TPT

SELF-CONTROL

Jumping out of an airplane sounds like it would be a chaotic experience, and to some, it's more than chaotic; it's terrifying. That's what it's like to live without the influence of Christ producing the fruit of self-control. When we live our lives with an "anything goes" attitude, it becomes a chaotic life, much like trying to jump out of an airplane without proper equipment and training. A life without self-control is like a nation without laws, complete anarchy. Self-control is not possible without the influence of Christ in our hearts, minds, and lives. Controlling our thoughts, emotions, words, and behaviors without Christ would be a burdensome and challenging task. He is the established standard, the one who exemplified how we should be. In these times, we must rely on God's Word to transform us, empower us, and strengthen us.

Heavenly Father, teach me through your Word to desire your will above my own. Take any unclean and unholy desire from my heart so I am in fellowship with your presence, producing the fruit of self-control in my life. Amen.

Knowing God's Word equips you to live a life of self-control. Living his Word empowers you to do this. How can your desires be changed by God's Word?

A person without self-control
is like a city with broken-down walls.

PROVERBS 25:28 NLT

For this very reason, make every effort to supplement your faith with goodness, goodness with knowledge, knowledge with self-control, self-control with endurance, endurance with godliness, godliness with brotherly affection, and brotherly affection with love. For if these qualities are yours and are increasing, they will keep you from being useless or unfruitful in the knowledge of our Lord Jesus Christ.

2 PETER 1:5–8 HCSB

STRENGTH

One of the most familiar Scripture passages on strength is Philippians 4:13, where Paul writes, "I can do all things through Christ who strengthens me" (NKJV). The Greek word for *strengthen* here means "to put power in." This verse isn't as much about accomplishing things in life, as it is often portrayed, as it is about allowing God to strengthen us by his spirit in times of hardship and times of abundance. We must learn to lean on his presence for strength in good times and in times of difficulty. As he sustained many throughout Scripture and in our time, he will sustain you as you continue to trust him and depend on his presence for strength. No matter the challenges you face in life, true strength isn't found in physical or mental ability to overcome a challenge. Rather, it is rooted in the resiliency of the spirit man who is led by the Holy Spirit.

Heavenly Father, thank you for your strength, which sustains me through all things. Amen.

Have you experienced the strength of God's presence in your life?

In your strength I can crush an army;
with my God I can scale any wall.

2 SAMUEL 22:30 NLT

The LORD is my strength and my song;
He has become my salvation.

PSALM 118:14 HCSB

Those who wait upon God get fresh strength.
They spread their wings and soar like eagles,
They run and don't get tired,
they walk and don't lag behind.

ISAIAH 40:29–30 MSG

I take pleasure in weaknesses, insults, catastrophes,
persecutions, and in pressures, because of Christ.
For when I am weak, then I am strong.

2 CORINTHIANS 12:10 HCSB

I know what it is to be in need, and I know what it is to
have plenty. I have learned the secret of being content
in any and every situation, whether well fed or hungry,
whether living in plenty or in want. I can do all this
through him who gives me strength.

PHILIPPIANS 4:12–13 NIV

TESTING

The word *test* in the Old Testament comes from the Hebrew word *bachan,* which means to "examine, try, prove." Fire is used by blacksmiths to test and mold iron, and it purifies precious metals. But God tests the heart. When we are presented with challenging circumstances, it can be tempting to take the easy way out, the path of least resistance, but this will not lead to a place of growing in faith and character in Christ. What God's testing of us proves is that he longs for us to grow in the knowledge of who he is, through his Word, in trusting him, and by deepening our faith. Just as you would be required to pass tests in school before advancing to the next level, you must pass tests in this life before being promoted with new gifts and opportunities. Don't overlook the small, seemingly insignificant tests, for sometimes they carry heavy weight. To grow and advance in the things of God, we must pass the difficult tests of life. Will your heart pass the test?

Heavenly Father, thank you for the tests. I trust in you and will lean on your understanding, not my own, so I no longer have to fear the tests that may come. Guide my steps, and I will find favor in your eyes. Amen.

You will face numerous tests in this life. Each day presents new tests. How does facing these tests with the right attitude and heart affect your life?

I will put this third through the fire; I will refine them as silver is refined and test them as gold is tested. They will call on My name, and I will answer them. I will say: They are My people, and they will say: Yahweh is our God.

ZECHARIAH 13:9 HCSB

No test or temptation that comes your way is beyond the course of what others have had to face. All you need to remember is that God will never let you down; he'll never let you be pushed past your limit; he'll always be there to help you come through it.

1 CORINTHIANS 10:13 MSG

He suffered and endured every test and temptation, so that he can help us every time we pass through the ordeals of life.

HEBREWS 2:18 TPT

TRUST

It is likely that you've dined at a restaurant at least once in your lifetime. However, chances are that you don't thoroughly examine the chairs before sitting in them. Why? Aren't you concerned about falling on the ground? You don't examine them because you trust the reliability of the builder, whom you do not know. You also trust the strength of the chair to hold you when you sit down, and you trust that since the chair is still positioned at the table, it is available for occupancy. We trust in chairs, but we are reluctant to trust in others, in ourselves, and even at times, in God. If the maker of the chairs, who is unknown to us, can be trusted, we can be even freer in trusting the Creator of the universe. He holds the stars in balance, and all the tomorrows he knows. Today, if things seem to be swirling out of control, trust in the one who holds everything in the palm of his hand. He is reliable, his strength will sustain, and he will not fail.

Heavenly Father, I know there are times I am not easily trusting of others or of you. I demonstrate this lack of trust through my thoughts, words, and actions. Today, I place my trust wholly in your hands. Amen.

In the middle of the most daunting places of life as a first responder, you know how trust between coworkers is critical to your success. How much more important is your trust in God through this life?

The LORD said to Moses and Aaron, "Because you did not trust me enough to demonstrate my holiness to the people of Israel, you will not lead them into the land I am giving them!"

NUMBERS 20:12 NLT

You keep all your promises. You are the Creator of heaven's glory, earth's grandeur, and ocean's greatness.

PSALM 146:6 TPT

To all the rich of this world, I command you not to be wrapped in thoughts of pride over your prosperity, or rely on your wealth, for your riches are unreliable and nothing compared to the living God. Trust instead in the one who has lavished upon us all good things, fulfilling our every need.

1 TIMOTHY 6:17 TPT

WISDOM

The fear demonstrated by a victim in the face of a threat of evil is not the type of fear mentioned in Psalm 111:10 when it says, "The fear of the LORD is the beginning of wisdom" (NKJV). One kind of fear is servile fear, a fear of someone who has power over you. The other type of fear, as mentioned in Psalm 111:10, is a filial fear: the respect and love you had for your parents when you were a child. The first is rooted in authority and the other in a relationship with God. Step one for obtaining God's wisdom is seeing him as our heavenly Father, then praying and earnestly desiring wisdom, and finally consistently studying the Bible. His wisdom changes everything, and having a relationship with God is step one of obtaining this life-changing gift he offers.

Heavenly Father, I come to you with a childlike faith because of your Son, Jesus. He has redeemed me. I ask you for wisdom above all things in this life, and I thank you for equipping me with an abundance of it now and always. Amen.

How does the wisdom of God guide you differently than human wisdom?

The fear of the LORD is the beginning of wisdom;
all who follow his precepts have good understanding.
To him belongs eternal praise.

PSALM 111:10 NIV

Getting wisdom is the wisest thing you can do!
And whatever else you do, develop good judgment.

PROVERBS 4:7 NLT

Wisdom will exalt you when you exalt her truth.
She will lead you to honor and favor when you
live your life by her insights.

PROVERBS 4:8 TPT

Men and women who have lived wisely and well will
shine brilliantly, like the cloudless, star-strewn night
skies. And those who put others on the right path to life
will glow like stars forever.

DANIEL 12:3 MSG

If any of you lacks wisdom, you should ask God,
who gives generously to all without finding fault,
and it will be given to you.

JAMES 1:5 NIV

WORKS

In the physical realm, one ultimate evil can undo a life-time of good. No matter how many good deeds and wonderful works you have done, if you unlawfully, willingly, and directly take the life of a single innocent person, then you could potentially spend the rest of your life in prison or possibly even face execution. This one "ultimate bad" of murder will undo all the good works in your life. No good deeds will be sufficient to overcome your guilt. But in the *spiritual* realm, one "perfect good" can undo a life-time of bad. The ultimate good of Jesus' sacrifice upon the cross to pay the price for our salvation saves us spir-itually, eternally. Think about that: every bad act in our lives—past, present, and future—is forgiven if we accept the price that Jesus paid upon the cross. We can and should do good deeds, giving the honor and glory to God and letting his love shine forth through our works, but we should never forget that it is not by our works but by the righteousness of Jesus and his sacrifice on the cross that we attain salvation.

Heavenly Father, I come to you and place all my works upon your altar, knowing that it is only through the sacrifice of Jesus that I am saved. I thank you for eternal life. In Jesus' holy name I pray. Amen.

How do your works impact your salvation?

If it is by grace, it is no longer on the basis of works;
otherwise grace would no longer be grace.

ROMANS 11:6 ESV

He saved us, not because of works done by us in
righteousness, but according to his own mercy, by the
washing of regeneration and renewal of the Holy Spirit.

TITUS 3:5 ESV

We know that a person is not justified by works of the
law but through faith in Jesus Christ, so we also have
believed in Christ Jesus, in order to be justified by faith
in Christ and not by works of the law, because by works
of the law no one will be justified.

GALATIANS 2:16 ESV

Let your light shine before others,
so that they may see your good works and give glory to
your Father who is in heaven.

MATTHEW 5:16 ESV

ACKNOWLEDGMENTS

The authors would like to extend a special thank you to the team at BroadStreet Publishing for their unrelenting support and commitment to first responders. We would also like to extend our gratitude to our families for their support and encouragement throughout the process of preparing and writing this book.

ABOUT THE AUTHORS

Adam Davis is an author, motivational speaker, and former law enforcement officer. His story reveals the pain that many hide and addresses topics that many avoid. Adam shares his experiences of sexual assault, substance abuse, mental illness, and the struggles and challenges of working in law enforcement. Adam is known for his work on *Behind the Badge: 365 Daily Devotions for Law Enforcement*, *Bulletproof Marriage: A 90-Day Devotional* (with Lt. Col. Dave Grossman), *and On Spiritual Combat: 30 Missions for Victorious Warfare* (with Lt. Col. Dave Grossman). *Bulletproof Marriage* was a finalist for the 2020 Christian Book Award®.

Adam's work has been featured in *Entrepreneur Magazine*, Fox News, *The Huffington Post,* PoliceOne.com, and Law Enforcement Today. As a speaker, he has presented for the University of Alabama, Auburn University Department of Economic Development, TEDx Troy University, law enforcement agencies, military bases, and many seminars with Lt. Col. Dave Grossman, Taya Kyle, and other American patriots. His media appearances have

included *The Rick & Bubba Show*, *The Blaze Radio Network*, *Family Life Today*, *The 700 Club*, *The Glenn Beck Program*, *Team Never Quit* podcast with Marcus Luttrell, and many others.

Today, Adam continues to dedicate his life to helping others navigate the challenges of marriage and overcoming adversity by continuing to author new, quality resources and speaking across the nation. You can stay up to date with Adam's events and new releases by visiting www.TheAdamDavis.com. He is proudly supported by his wife of twenty years, Amber, and three children.

In their description of Lt. Col. Dave Grossman (US Army Retired), *Slate Magazine* said, "Grossman cuts such a heroic, omnicompetent figure, he could have stepped out of a video game." He has five patents to his name and has published four novels, two children's books, and six nonfiction books to include his "perennial bestseller" *On Killing* (with over half a million copies sold), and a *New York Times* bestselling book coauthored with Glenn Beck.

He is a US Army Ranger, a paratrooper, and a former West Point Psychology Professor. He has a Black Belt in Hojutsu, the martial art of the firearm, and has been inducted into the USA Martial Arts Hall of Fame.

Col. Grossman's research was cited by the President of the United States in a national address, and he has testified before the US Senate, the US Congress, and numerous state legislatures. He has served as an expert witness and consultant in both state and federal courts. He helped train mental health professionals after the Jonesboro school massacre, and he was also involved in counseling or court cases in the aftermath of the Paducah, Springfield, Littleton, and Nickel Mines Amish school massacres.

Col. Grossman has been called upon to write the entry on "Aggression and Violence" in the Oxford Companion to American Military History and three entries in the Academic Press Encyclopedia of Violence, Peace, and Conflict and has presented papers before the national conventions of the American Medical Association, the American Psychiatric Association, the American Psychological Association, and the American Academy of Pediatrics.

Since his retirement from the US Army in 1998, he has been on the road almost three hundred days a year, for over nineteen years, as one of our nation's leading trainers for military, law enforcement, mental health providers, and school safety organizations.

Today Col. Grossman is the director of the Killology Research Group (www.killology.com). In the wake of the 9/11 terrorist attacks he has written and spoken extensively on the terrorist threat, with articles published in the Harvard Journal of Law and Civil Policy and many leading law enforcement journals, and he has been inducted as a Life Diplomate by the American Board for Certification in Homeland Security and a Life Member of the American College of Forensic Examiners Institute.